REFINE YOUR

FINANCE

Master Budgeting and Build Wealth for a Secure Future

By

J KHAN

Table Of Contents

Introduction

In today's fast-paced world, financial literacy has never been more crucial. Whether you're student stepping into the professional world, a seasoned employee or an entrepreneur, understanding the nuances of finance is a key to make informed decisions that shape your future.

Yet, despite the overwhelming influence of finance in our daily lives, many people remain unaware of how to effectively manage their money, invest for the future or plan for unexpected financial challenges.

This book aims to demystify the world of finance, breaking down complex concepts into practical advice that anyone can apply to their own financial journey. Through this book, we aim to empower readers with the tools and knowledge necessary to take control of their financial destiny.

Personal finance is more than just budgeting and saving- it's about understanding the broader financial systems, making smart investment choices and cultivating habits that lead to long term financial well being.

The principles and strategies presented here have been crafted with the understanding that everyone's financial situation is unique and there is no one size fits all solution.

Whether you're looking to eliminate debt, grow your savings or plan for retirement, the insight within these pages are designed to equip you with the confidence and knowledge to make financial decisions that align with your goals. Finance in its essence is not about numbers, it's about freedom and peace of mind that comes from taking charge of financial future.

STORY

Arjun and Vikram were childhood friends, both working in the same company, earning the same salary. However, their approach to money was starkly different and it soon became evident in their financial journeys.

Arjun was disciplined about his finances. He understood the importance of budgeting and saving, so he lived within the means. Arjun started investing in mutual funds and stocks with a small portion of his salary. He also focused on building an emergency fund and paid off his student loans early. Over the time his saving grew and his investment began yielding returns. With patience and consistent effort, Arjun achieved financial freedom. He was no longer worried about bills or unexpected expenses and could plan for future goals like travel, early retirement and buying a house without financial stress.

On the other hand, Vikram was caught up in a cycle of instant gratification. He spent his salary on luxury items, dining out and the latest gadget, even though he couldn't afford them. He used credit cards to cover his expenses, quickly accumulating debt instead of saving or investing. He took out personal loans to maintain his lifestyle, digging himself deeper into financial hole. With high interest rates and growing bills, Vikram found himself struggling to make ends meet each month.

Despite earning the same salary, Arjun's financial discipline allowed him to thrive, while Vikram's lack of planning trapped him in a never-ending cycle of debt. Their stories serve as a powerful reminder that financial freedom isn't determine by income alone but by how we manage and grow our money.

Budgeting

"Budgeting is not just about balancing numbers; it's about balancing your priorities and creating the freedom to live the life you want."

Budgeting for monthly expenses in India can be a great way to manage your finances and ensure you are able to save and meet your financial goals. Here's a step by step guide on how to effectively budget for your monthly expenses :

1. Track Your Income

Start by identifying all sources of income. This can include salary, freelance work, investments, or any other regular sources of money. Make sure to account for the net income (after tax deductions) rather than gross income.

2. List Your Monthly Expenses

Break down your monthly expenses into categories. Some common ones might include:

- **Fixed Expenses**: These are predictable and consistent, such as rent, utility bill (electricity, water, gas), EMI on loans, insurance premium etc.

- **Variable Expenses**: These may fluctuate each month, such as groceries, transportation, fuel and entertainment.

- **Discretionary Expenses**: Expenses that are not necessary but still part of your lifestyle like dining out, shopping, subscription etc

3. Categorize and Prioritize Your Expenses

Categorize your expenses into essential (needs) and non-essential (wants). For example:

- **Needs**: Rent, groceries, utilities, medical expenses etc

- **Wants**: Eating out, entertainment, vacations or buying gadgets.

4. Create a Budgeting Plan

50/30/20 Rule: A popular budgeting rule is to divide your income as follows:

- **50% for Needs**: These include rent, groceries, transportation and bills.

- **30% for Wants**: These include entertainment, vacations, buying gadgets.

- **20% for savings & Debt Repayment**: These include Saving, investments (eg PPF, mutual funds or SIPs) or paying of any debts.

You can adjust these percentages depending on your financial priorities.

5. Plan for Savings

- **Emergency Fund:** Its important to have at least 3-6 months of living expenses saved up for emergencies.

- **Investment:** Consider setting aside a portion of your income for long term goals like retirement, buying a home or education. Look into different investment options like mutual funds, stocks and fixed deposits.

- **Automatic Transfer:** To make saving a habit, set up automatic transfers to your saving account or investment account on the day you receive your salary.

6. Control Your Spending

- **Track Spending:** Use apps or spreadsheet to track every expense. This will help you realize where you're overspending.

- **Cutting Unnecessary Expenses:** Look for areas where you can cut down. For instance, you could reduce dining out, limit impulse purchases or find cheaper alternatives for things like transportation.

7. Use Budgeting Apps

There are many apps available that can help you track expenses. Some popular apps include:

- **Walnut:** Help you to track spending and manage budgets

- **Money View**: Tracks expenses, provides insight and helps create a budget.

- **Monefy**: Easy to use app for tracking expenses and setting budget goals

8. Avoid Debt

- Be cautious about taking on too much debt. If you have existing debt, prioritize paying it off to avoid high-interest payments

- If you need a loan, consider options that offers lower interest rates, such as a personal loan or home loan and make sure you can comfortably afford the EMI.

9. Be Disciplined

Finally, the key to successful budgeting is discipline. Stick to your budget as closely as possible and make adjustments if necessary, but avoid unnecessary splurges or deviations from your plan.

Example of a Simple Budget Breakdown:

Assume a monthly income of ₹ 50000/-

50% for Needs (₹ 25000)

- Rent: ₹10000/-

- Utilities: ₹ 3000/-

- Groceries₹6000/-

- Transportation: ₹ 2000/-

- Insurance premiums: ₹ 4000/-

30% for Wants (₹ 15000)

- Dining Out: ₹ 4000/-

- Entertainment (movies, event): ₹ 3000/-

- Subscription(Netflix, gym etc): ₹ 2000/-

- Shopping: ₹ 6000/-

20% for Savings (₹ 10000)

- Emergency Fund: ₹ 5000/-

- Investment(PPF/Mutual Funds): ₹ 5000/-

By following this process, you can create solid foundation for your financial health and start working towards your financial goals.

KEY TAKE AWAY

- Divide Your Income as per 50/30/20 Rule

- Track Your Spending

- Prioritize Needs Over Wants

- Build an Emergency Fund

- Review and Adjust Regularly

INFLATION

"INFLATION *IS TAXATION WITHOUT LEGISLATION*"

Inflation in India refers to the rate at which the prices of goods and services increase over time, reducing the purchasing power of the currency. It is a key economic indicator that directly impacts the cost of living, economic growth, and standard of living for millions of people. Inflation in India has been a recurring challenge, often fluctuating due to a combination of domestic and global factors

Inflation can be attributed to various factors both domestic and global that influence the rise in prices of Goods and Services. The key reasons for inflation are

1. Demand-Pull Inflation

This type of inflation occurs when aggregate demand exceeds aggregate supply in the economy. It is often driven by:

- **Increased consumer spending**: Rising incomes, urbanization and a growing middle class contribute to higher consumer demand, particularly for non-essential and luxury goods.

- **Government expenditure**: Large government spending on infrastructure, welfare or defense can create an increased in overall demand in the economy

- **Low-interest rates**: When the Reserve Bank of India (RBI) lower interest rates, borrowing becomes cheaper leading to higher spending by businesses and consumer, which increases demand.

2. Cost–Push Inflation

Cost push inflation occurs when the cost of production increases; leading business   to pass on higher costs to consumers. This is typically caused by:

- **Increased in fuel prices**: India is a net importer of crude oil and fluctuation in   global fuel prices directly impact domestic fuel prices. Rising oil prices increase transportation and production costs, causing the prices of a wide range of goods to rise.

- **Wage hikes**: If wages in key sectors (agriculture, manufacturing and services) rise, businesses may increase prices to compensate for higher labour costs

- **Raw material price increases**: Higher costs for raw materials such as metals or food ingredients lead to increased prices in manufacturing and agriculture products.

3. Supply Chain Disruptions

India is a part of a globalized economy and any disruption in supply chains both domestic and international can lead to inflationary pressures. Key causes include:

- **Natural Disasters:** Poor monsoons, floods or draughts can disrupt agriculture production, especially in rural areas. For example crop failure lead to shortage of staple food like rice, wheat and vegetable pushing their prices up.

- **Geopolitical events:** War, trade conflict or political instability can affect the supply of critical goods and commodities such as crude oil, metals and food products. Any disruption in the supply of these goods can lead to higher prices.

- **Pandemics:** As seen with the covid-19 pandemic, disruption to production, transportation and logistics can lead to shortages, higher costs and ultimately, inflation

4. Monetary Policy and Money Supply

The Reserve Bank of India controls inflation indirectly through its monetary policy. The most common way this happens is through the supply of money in the economy.

- **Expansionary monetary policy**: When the RBI lowers interest rates, borrowing becomes cheaper which can increase spending boosts demands for goods and services which can lead to demand-pull inflation.

- Excess money policy: If the RBI prints more money or keeps interest rates too low for too long, too much money in the economy can lead to an increase in demand causing prices to rise. An increase in money supply without a corresponding increase in the supply of goods and services results in inflation.

5. Global Commodity Price Fluctuations

India is a significant importer of key commodities such as oil, metals and agriculture products. Fluctuation in global commodity prices can have a direct impact on domestic inflation. For example:

- **Oil prices**: India imports a substantial amount of crude oil, and any rise in global oil prices leads to higher cost for transportation, manufacturing and energy, which in turn increases the overall price of goods and services in the economy

- Food and agriculture prices: India is also reliant in imports for various food items like pulses, edible oils and other essentials. A rise in international food prices often due to weather conditions, trade policies or geopolitical tensions can lead to higher food inflation in India.

6. Supply Chain Disruptions

Agriculture is a vital sector in India employing a large proportion of the population. The country heavily depends on seasonal agriculture production. Variability in the monsoon or poor agriculture productivity can cause food inflation, one of the primary drivers of overall inflation in India:

- **Monsoon dependency**: A deficient monsoon can result in lower crop yields, leading to shortages in essential food items like cereals, pulses and vegetables. When food supply is limited, prices increase.

- **Storage and transportation issues**: India's inadequate cold storage and transportation infrastructure can lead to spoilage, wastage and price hikes, especially for perishable items.

7. Currency Depreciation

A weakening of the Indian Rupee against major currencies like US Dollar can lead to inflation by making imports more expensive. This is especially true for commodities like oil which India imports in large quantities.

- **Oil and energy imports**: Since India imports most of its oil, a depreciation in the Rupee makes oil more expensive, increasing fuel costs and subsequently the price of goods and services dependent on transportation and energy.

- **Imports goods and raw materials**: A weaker Rupee increases the cost of imported raw material, which raises production costs and can lead to higher prices for domestically manufactured goods.

EFFECTS OF INFLATION ON ECONOMY

Inflation in India has several significant effects on the economy and the lives of its citizens. Here are some of the key impacts:

- **Reduced purchasing power**: Inflation erodes the purchasing power of money, meaning people can buy less with the same amount of money. The effects house -holds, particularly those with fixed incomes, as they struggle to maintain the standard of living.

- **Rising Cost of Living**: with inflation, the prices of goods and services, including food, transportation and healthcare rise. This increase the cost of living, making it harder for people to meet basic needs.

- **Impact on Saving**: Inflation discourages saving because the value for money dismisses over time. People may prefer to spend rather than save, as the real value of saving decrease with high inflation.

- **Increased Interest Rates**: To combat inflation, the Reserve Bank India (RBI) often raises interest rates. While this helps control inflation, it also makes loans more expensive for consumers and businesses, slowing down economic activity.

- **Wage Pressure**: As the cost of living increases, workers may demand higher wages to keep up the inflation. If wage increases do not keep pace with inflation, it can lead to a decline in real wages.

- **Income Inequality:** Inflation tends to disproportionately affect low-income groups because they spend a higher percentage of their income on necessities, such as food and housing. As the prices of these goods rise, the burden on low-income families increases.

- **Investment Uncertainty:** High inflation can create uncertainty in the economy, making it difficult for businesses to plan for the future, as companies hesitate to make long term commitments due to unpredictable cost.

- **Export and Imports: Inflation can** affect the competitiveness of India's exports. If inflation in India is higher than in other countries, Indian goods become more expensive abroad, which could reduce demand for them. On the other hand, the cost of imports may rise, leading to trade imbalance.

HOW A COMMON MAN CAN BEAT INFLATION

1. **Financial Planning & Budgeting**

   - **Track Spending**: A key step in managing personal finances is tracking expenses and reducing unnecessary spending. Prioritize needs over wants.

   - **Budgeting**: Creating a monthly budget helps in controlling expenditure and plan for future needs.

2. **Invest in Inflation- Protected Assets:**

   - **Invest in stocks or mutual funds**: Stock and equities often outperform inflation in the long run, although they carry risks. Investing in equity-based mutual funds can be a good strategy

- **Gold**: Gold is considered a hedge against inflation. Investing in gold or gold ETFs can preserve value over time.

- **Inflation-Linked Bonds**: Government –issued bonds that are linked to inflation can offer protection by providing returns that keep pace with inflation.

3. Increase Income

- **Side Jobs or Freelancing**: Take up additional work, such as freelancing or part time jobs, to supplement your primary income.

- **Upskill or Reskill**: Invest in learning new skills or certification that can increase your earning potential and make you more competitive in the job market.

- **Entrepreneurship**: Consider starting a small business or side hustle, which can provide an additional source of income.

4. Save Smartly

- **Emergency Fund:** Build and maintain an emergency fund to cover unexpected expenses. This fund can act as a cushion when inflation reduces purchasing power.

- **High-Interest saving Accounts**: Use saving accounts or fixed deposits with higher interest rates to make your saving work for you.

5. Switch to Cheaper Alternatives

- **Generic Brands**: Choose store brands or generic products over premium brands, as they are often just as effective but much cheaper.

- **Bulk Buying**: Purchase items in bulk, especially non-perishable goods, to save money in the long run.

- **Energy Saving Measures**: Reduce electricity consumption by switching to energy-efficient appliances, using less heating/cooling and turning off devices when not in use.

6. Avoid Debt

- **Minimize Borrowing:** High-Interest loans and credit card debt can become more expensive when inflation rises. Avoid taking unnecessary debt, especially for non-essential items.

- **Pay Off Existing Debt:** Focus on paying off high-interest debt (such as credit card) quickly to reduce financial strain

7. Shop Smart

- **Take advantage of Sales:** Buy items during sales, festivals or discount seasons. Use coupons, cashback offers and loyality points to lower costs

- **Buy Second-Hand:** Consider purchasing second-hand items for big ticket purchase like furniture or electronics. Many second hand items are in excellent condition and much cheaper.

8. Focus on Health

- **Preventive Care:** Instead of waiting for health issues to arise, focus on maintaining good health through exercise and proper nutrition. This can help reduce long-term healthcare costs.

By following these strategies, a common person can minimize the impact of inflation on their finances, protect their purchasing power and even grow their wealth in challenging economic times.

KEY TAKE AWAY

- Inflation raises prices

- Erodes saving

- Wages lag behind inflation

- Invest in inflation-resistant assets

- Reduce discretionary spending & diversify investment

Power Of Compounding

"Compound interest is the eighth wonder of the world. He who understand it, earns it, he who doesn't, pays it"

- Albert Einstein

The Power of Compounding: A Key to Wealth Creation

The power of compounding is often referred to as one of the most powerful concepts in finance. It is the principle where the returns on an investment or saving earn their own return over time, leading to exponential growth. While it may seem slow initially with time, compounding turns modest investment into significant wealth.

What is Compounding?

At its core, compounding is earning returns on both the original investment (the principal) and the accumulated interest or earnings. This "interest on interest" is what makes compounding so powerful.

For example: if you invest ₹ 10000/- at an annual interest rate of 10%, at the end of the first year, you will have ₹ 11000 (₹ 10000 principal + ₹ 1000 interest). In the second year, you will earn interest on ₹ 11000, resulting in ₹ 1100 in interest. This cycle continues and the longer you stay invested, the greater the impact of your compounding.

Data and Facts about Power of Compounding

1. **Time is the key Factor**: The earlier you start, the more time your money has to grow. Compounding work best over long periods.

2. **Small Contribution Matter**: Even small, consistent contribution can add up significantly due to compounding. For instance, investing ₹ 6000/- every month in a mutual fund that earns an average annual return of 12% can result in ₹ 55 lakh in 20 years. If you increase your same contribution by 10% every year with the same time period, then you will get ₹ 1 crore 11 lakh and 90 thousand.

3. **The 72 Rule**: A quick way to estimate how long it will take for your investment to double is the rule of 72. Divide 72 by the annual rate of return to get the numbers of years it will take for your money to double. For example, if you invest at 8% return, it will take approximately **9 years** for your investment to double (72/8=9).

Example: Power of Compounding in Action

Let's look at real-world example to understand compounding better.

Scenario:

Imagine you are a 25 years old and you start investing ₹ 5000/- every month in a mutual fund that provides an average annual return of 12%. You continue to this investment until you turn 60.

- Initial investment: ₹ 5000/- per month

- Annual Return: 12%

- Investment period: 35 years

Using the formulae, after 35 years, your investment will grow to approximately

₹ 2.75 crore. However, if you had started at 20 years of your age, your return on investment would be ₹ 4.90 crore. This shows how just adding 5 more years in your investment and let the compounding work, its magic can significantly increase your wealth.

How One Can Use the Power of Compounding to Build your Wealth

1. **Start Early:** One of the most significant advantages you can have is time. If individual investors start investing in their 20s, they can leverage compounding for longer period, building substantial wealth.

2. **Invest in High-Return Assets:** To make the most of compounding, consider investing in instruments that offer higher returns that traditional savings account.

3. **Systematic Investment Plans (SIPs):** SIPs are an excellent way to harness the power of compounding. By contributing a fixed amount regularly, an investor

takes advantage of rupee cost averaging, reducing the impact of market volatility. Over time, the money grows exponentially as interest is earned on both the principal and the accumulated earnings.

4. **Reinvest Dividends and Interest:** Another way to benefit from compounding is by reinvesting any dividends or interest earned from your investment. For example, if you invest in dividend-paying stocks or mutual funds, reinvesting the dividends will allow your money to grow at an even faster rate.

5. **Diversify your Investments:** To take full advantage of compounding, it's important to diversify your portfolio. By investing in a mix of equities, debt instrument, real estate and other assets, you reduce risk and maximize potential returns. Diversification ensures that you continue to earn compound returns across different asset classes.

6. **Avoid Withdrawals:** The key to benefiting from compound is to let your investments grow without interruption. Regular withdrawal will interrupt the compounding process. It's essential to have a long-term view and remain patient as compounding only becomes powerful over time.

The power of compounding is the key to building wealth over time, especially for Indian investors. Starting early, consistently investing and allowing your investments to grow without disruption can turn modest contributions into substantial wealth. Whether through SIPs, high return asset, or reinvest dividends, the ability to leverage compounding can pave the way for financial independence and a comfortable future. The longer you let your money compound, the larger your wealth can grow- so start today!

KEY TAKE AWAY

- Compounding enables money to grow exponentially

- The longer the period, the greater the benefit

- Small contribution, Big impact

- Reinvest to maximizes returns

- Patience pays off

Insurance

"The best time to buy insurance is before you need it"

UNDERSTANDING INSURANCE: Insurance is a financial safety net that provides protection against potential financial losses caused by unexpected events. Whether its health issues, accidents or damage to property, insurance can shield individuals and families from the devastating financial impact of such events. There are various types of insurance tailored to meet different needs and understanding these options is crucial for safeguarding your financial future.

Type of insurance

1. **Health Insurance:** Health insurance is designed to cover the costs associated with medical care. It helps individuals and families manage expenses related to hospitalization, surgeries, doctor visits, medications and other healthcare services. Health insurance plans can be divided into:

   - **Individual Health Insurance:** Covers a single person's medical expenses.

   - **Family Floater Health Insurance:** A plan that covers the medical expenses of an entire family under one policy.

- **Critical Illness Insurance:** Provides coverage specifically for life threatening conditions such as cancer, heart disease or stroke.

- **Top Up Plans:** Additional coverage over existing health plan to cover larger hospital bills.

2. **Auto Insurance:** Auto insurance protects vehicle owner from financial losses due to accidents, theft, natural disasters or vandalism. In India having at least third party insurance is mandatory. Auto insurance plan include:

   - **Third –Party Insurance:** It covers damage or injury caused to third   parties (other vehicles, people or property) by your vehicle.

   - **Comprehensive Insurance:** It covers both third-party damage as well as damage to your own vehicle.

   - **Own Damage Insurance:** Provides coverage for damage to your vehicle caused by accident, fire, theft or natural calamities.

3. **Life Insurance:** Life insurance provides financial support to the policyholder's family or beneficiaries in the event of their death. It ensures that loved ones don't face financial struggles due to the loss of the primary breadwinner. Life insurance plans can include:

   - **Term Life Insurance:** Provides coverage for a specified period and pays the sum assured to beneficiaries if the policy holder passes away during that term

- **Whole Life Insurance:** Offers lifelong coverage and provides both a death benefit and a cash value accumulation over time.

- **Endowment Plans:** Combines life insurance with a savings component offering a payout either upon death or after the policy term ends.

4. **Home Insurance:** Home insurance covers damages to your house and its contents due to events like fire, theft, natural disasters, or accidents. It helps in repair, replacements and even temporary accommodation if necessary.

5. **Travel Insurance:** Travel insurance is designed to protect individuals while travelling, offering coverage for trip cancellations, lost luggage, emergency and other travel related risks.

Understanding First Party, Second Party and Third Party Insurance

1. **First Party Insurance:** The first party is the policy holder or the person buying the insurance policy. This is the individual or entity seeking protection against risks

2. **Second Party Insurance:** The second party refers to the insurance company that is providing coverage and taking the premium payments from the policyholder. In shorts, the insurance company is the second party in this agreement,

3. **Third Party Insurance:** Third party insurance refers to insurance that covers damages caused to other (not the policy holder). For example, in auto insurance, the policyholder is the first party, and the other person involved in the accident is the third party. Third party insurance helps to protect the policyholder from financial liability for damages or injuries caused to the third party.

For instance, if you accidentally hit someone else's car, third-party insurance would cover the damage to the other's car, as well as any medical costs or damage to their property.

Here is an estimate chart to show how much life insurance might be required based on income and family situation.

Income Level (INR)	Single (No Dependent)	Married (No Children)	Married (With Children)
Up to ₹ 5,00,000	₹ 25,00,000- ₹ 35,00,000	₹ 35,00,000- ₹ 50,00,000	₹ 50,00,000- ₹ 75,00,000
₹ 5,00,000- ₹ 10,00,000	₹ 25,00,000- ₹ 35,00,000	₹ 35,00,000- ₹ 60,00,000	₹ 60,00,000- ₹ 1,00,00,000
₹ 5,00,000- ₹ 10,00,000	₹ 5,00,000- ₹ 10,00,000	₹ 5,00,000- ₹ 10,00,000	₹ 60,00,000- ₹ 1,00,00,000
₹ 10,00,000- ₹ 25,00,000	₹ 30,00,000- ₹ 50,00,000	₹ 50,00,000- ₹ 1,00,00,000	₹ 1,00,00,000- ₹ 2,00,00,000
₹ 25,00,000- ₹ 50,00,000	₹ 35,00,000- ₹ 60,00,000	₹ 60,00,000- ₹ 1,20,00,000	₹ 1,50,00,000- ₹ 3,00,00,000

Key Points to Keep in Mind While Taking Insurance (LIFE / VEHICLE)

1. **Evaluate Your Needs:** Before buying insurance, assess your needs. A young, healthy person might need basic health coverage while someone with a family and dependents might need a more comprehensive policy.

2. **Understand coverage:** Thoroughly read and understand what is covered under the policy. For example many auto insurance policies might not cover natural disasters unless explicitly stated.

3. **Compare Premium:** Insurance premium can vary significantly between providers. It's essential to shop around and compare premiums while considering the level of coverage.

4. **Check Deductibles:** The deductible is the amount you pay out of pockets before the insurance company pays. Higher deductibles usually mean lower premiums, but you should ensure you can afford the deductibles in case of claim.

5. **Check IDV:** The Insured Declared Value (IDV) is the maximum amount an insurance company will pay you in case your vehicle is damaged beyond repair or stolen. It represents the current market value of the vehicle at the time policy is issued after considering depreciation.

6. **Claim Process:** Understand the process for filling a claim. Make sure you are comfortable with the documentation required and the timelines involved.

7. **Policy Term and Conditions:** Read the fine print, including any exclusion or limits on coverage. Certain situations or accidents caused by reckless driving may not be covered.

8. **Check CSR:** The Claim Settlement Ratio (CSR) is an important metric used to evaluate an insurance company's performance in settling claims. It is the percentage of the claims an insurer successfully settles compared to the total number of claims received in a specific period. A higher CSR indicates that the insurer is more likely to honor its policy holder's claim which is good indicator of reliability and trustworthiness.

9. **Free Look Period:** Free Look Period is a provision in insurance policies that allows policy holders to review the terms and conditions of their insurance policy after purchasing it. This period typically lasts between 15 to 30 days depending on the insurer and the region.

10. **Review Regularly:** Regularly review your insurance policies to ensure they still meet your needs, especially if you experience major life changes like marriage, having children or changing jobs.

11. **Don't mix Insurance with Investing:** Insurance is meant for protection, not investment. The returns from insurance policies are often very low. Relying on

insurance for investment can limit growth and flexibility in financial plan.

Insurance provides a safety net in times of financial hardship due to unexpected events. From health and auto insurance to life and home coverage having the right policy can help you to protect yourself and loved ones. Understanding the types of insurance available and knowing how to evaluate them is the key to making informed decisions.

KEY TAKE AWAY

- Insurance provides a safety net

- Select a policy that fits your need and risk profile

- Always read the fine print to understand what's covered and what's excluded in your policy to avoid surprise while claiming

- Find a balance between premium costs and coverage

- Review your insurance policies periodically

CREDIT CARDS

"Credit cards are like a gun: You either use it or it uses you."

A credit card is a financial tool that allows a consumer to borrow money from a lender, typically a bank or a credit card company to make purchases or withdraw cash with the promise to repay the borrowed amount, often with interest within a specified time frame. It is widely used around the globe for various purposes providing both consumers and businesses with flexible and convenient way to manage payments.

The history of credit cards dates back to the early 20th century, they have become an essential part of modern finance, influencing everything from global economies to individual credit scores.

The credit card industry has evolved significantly since its inception with various features, rewards and benefits aimed at making it an indispensable part of daily life for millions.

History of Credit Cards

The journey of the modern credit card began in the early 20th century when charge cards were first introduced, but it was in the 1950s that the concept of credit cards, as we know them today, truly began to take shape.

The first recognizable precursor to the credit card was the **Diners Club card** , introduced in 1950 by Frank

McNamara, who wanted to make it easier to pay for meals at restaurant without carrying cash. The idea quickly gained traction and soon other businesses began to offer similar services. However this was more of a charge card, which require the balance to be paid in full at the end of each billing cycle.

In 1958, American Express issued its first true credit card which allowed users to carry a balance from month to month and pay it off gradually with interest applied to the outstanding balance. This innovation opened the door to what would become a multi-billion-dollar industry. Shortly thereafter in 1959, **Bank of America** introduced the first **BankAmericard** which was later renames **Visa**, Following this, **Mastercard** emerged in 1966, when group of banks joined forces to create a competitor to BankAmericard. The introduction of these companies led to widespread adoption of credit cards in the United States, and by the 1970s, they were increasingly common in other countries.

The 1980s and 1990s saw further improvement, such as introduction of magnetic strips which allowed for more secure and convenient transactions. By the turn of the 21st century electronic payments and online shopping further accelerated the use of credit cards. Modern cards now come with various benefits such as loyalty programs, cashback and travel perks making them even more attractive to consumers. Today credit cards are issued by numerous financial institutions worldwide and the industry continues to grow with innovations in digital payments and contactless technology

Pros and Cons of Credit Cards

Pros:

1. **Convenience:** Credit cards offer unmatched convenience. They eliminate the need to carry large sums of cash and make payments quick and easy whether shopping in-store or online. Credit cards also facilitate international travel as they are widely accepted around the world.

2. **Building Credit History:** Using a credit card responsibly-by making timely payments and keeping credit utilization low-helps build a positive credit history, which can be beneficial when applying for loans or mortgages in the future.

3. **Reward and Perks:** Many credit cards offer various rewards programs, including cash-back, travel points and discounts. These rewards can add significant value especially if the cardholder uses the credit card for everyday purchases.

4. **Fraud protection:** Credit card companies typically provide strong fraud protection, including zero liability policies that protect users in case their card is lost or stolen. Many credit cards also offer purchase protection, extending warranties on product bought.

5. **Grace Periods and Flexibility:** Many credit cards offer a grace period which allows cardholders to pay off their balance in full without incurring interest charges. Additionally credit cards provide flexibility in

payment, enabling consumers to manage their finances more effectively.

Cons:

1. **High-Interest Rates:** One of the biggest drawback of credit cards is the high-interest rates charged on outstanding balances. If a cardholder carries a balance month to month, they can end up paying significantly more than the original amount borrowed due to interest and fees.

2. **Debt Accumulation:** Credit cards can make it easy for individuals to overspend. Without discipline this can lead to debt accumulation, which may be difficult to pay off. Unpaid balances can lead to high-interest charges, creating a cycle of debt.

3. **Annual Fees and Hidden Charges:** Many credit cards charge annual fees or have other hidden charges for certain services. Some cards also charges fee for late payments, foreign transactions or exceeding the credit limit, adding to the overall cost of using the card.

4. **Impact on Credit score:** If a person uses a credit card irresponsibly, such as maxing out their credit limit or missing payments, it can have a negative impact on their credit score, making it harder to qualify for loans or mortgages in the future.

5. **Fraud Risks:** While credit card companies provide fraud protection, there are still risks of identity theft

and fraudulent charges, particularly in the digital space. Consumer need to be vigilant about securing their card details and monitoring transactions

Who Should Take a Credit Card?

Credit cards are suitable for individuals who can manage their finances responsibly and have a stable source of income. People, who pay their bills on time, keep their credit utilization low (ideally under 30%) and avoid overspending, can benefit the most from credit cards.

Young adults starting to build their credit card history can also use credit cards wisely to establish a positive credit score. However, credit cards may not be ideal for individuals who have difficulty controlling their spending or have a history of poor financial management. Those prone to accumulating debt or missing payments should be cautious when considering credit cards. Credit card would be very useful if its reward points can match your shopping and travelling lifestyle.

HOW BANK BENEFIT FROM CREDIT CARDS

Bank benefit from issuing credit cards in several ways:

1. **Interest Charges**: One of the primary sources of revenue for banks comes from the interest charged on outstanding credit card balances. If the cardholder carries a balance, the bank earns interest at rates often higher than those of traditional loans, providing a profitable revenue stream.

2. **Annual Fees and Charges**: Many credit cards come with annual fees, which contribute to the bank income. Additionally bank charge fees for late payments, foreign transactions and exceeding the credit limit all of which add to their revenue.

3. **Merchant Fees**: When a consumer uses their credit card for transaction the merchant pays for a transaction the merchant pays a fees to the card-issuing bank. This merchant transaction fee (typically ranging from 1% to 3% per transaction) is another significant source of income for banks.

4. **Cross-Selling Opportunities:** Credit cards are often linked to other financial products like personal loans, insurance and saving accounts. Bank can use credit card customers as a base for cross-selling these products further enhancing their profits.

5. **Data and Insights:** By analyzing the spending patterns of credit card holders, bank can gain valuable insight into consumer behavior enabling them to designs, targeted marketing campaigns, improve customer retention and launch new products that cater to customer preferences.

In India, the growth of digital payments, the government's push towards cashless transaction and the increasing middle-class population have all contributed to the rise in credit card adoption. As a result banks are eager to issue credit cards to cater to this growing demand.

Manufacturing Companies of Credit Cards

Credit cards themselves are physically manufactured by specialized companies, with **VISA, MasterCard and American Express** being the dominant brands that issue the payment networks and standards for the cards.

These organizations are not directly involved in the production of the physical cards but set the infrastructure for the transaction and security features associated with them.

The actual production of the credit card is carried out by companies like **Gemalto** (now part of Thales,) **Entrust** and **IDEMIA** which specialize in secure card manufacturing.

These companies are responsible for embedding the security features such as microchips, magnetic strips and other elements that ensure the card is both functional and secure.

Credit cards are a cornerstone of modern financial systems, offering a range of benefits and risks. With responsible use they can be powerful tools for building credit, earning rewards and making purchases conveniently.

Banks globally have capitalized on the potential of credit cards, benefitting from interest charges, fees and merchant transaction charges. However it is essential for consumers to use credit card wisely to avoid financial pitfalls.

KEY TAKE AWAY

- Use credit card with responsibility

- Always pay off your balance in full

- Choose a cards that align with your spending habits to maximize benefits

- Credit card often offer better fraud protection than debit cards

- Maintaining a low credit utilization rate is key to maintaining a healthy credit score

LOAN

"Loans can either be a ladder to success or a chain to financial distress- choose wisely"

Early Beginnings

The origins of loans can be traced back to ancient civilizations, long before the establishment of modern banking systems in Mesopotamia, Greece and Rome, loans were based on trade agreement where individuals could borrow goods or money in exchange for repayment with interest.

The concept of interest bearing loans known as usury, started taking shape during this period. While charging interest was initially considered morally wrong, it was gradually accepted and become institutionalized in many societies.

In India, records of lending and borrowing practices date back to the Vedic period (circa 1500 BCE -500 BCE). The Arthashastra, an ancient Indian treatise on economic and statecraft, written by Kautilya, contains references loans and credit systems. During the Medieval period the banking system in India developed further with money lenders and merchants providing credit to individuals and business.

The Emergence of Modern Banking

Modern banking, as we know it, begins to take shape in Europe in the 17th century. The establishment of the Bank of

England in 1694 was a turning point in the formalization of banking systems, as it introduced concepts like central banking, regulation and standardized lending practices.

Over time, these practices spread globally, leading to the formation of financial institutions that could lend money to individuals, businesses and governments.

In India, the establishment of the first commercial bank, the Bank of Hindustan in 1770 marked the beginning of a formalized banking system. The Reserve Bank of India (RBI) established in 1935, brought further regulation and oversight to the Indian financial system, ensuring that lending activities were managed efficiently and safely.

Types of Loans

Loans can be broadly classified into various categories based on their purpose, security and terms. Below are some of the most common types of loans available:

1. Secured Loans

Secured loans are loans in which the borrower pledges as asset (like property or vehicle) as collateral. If the borrower defaults on repayment, the lender can seize the asset to recover the loan amount. These loans typically offer lower interest rates due to the reduced risk to the lender.

Examples:

- **Home Loans (Mortgage Loans)**: These loans allow individuals to purchase homes or properties by borrowing funds from banks. The property serves as collateral for the loan.

- **Car Loan**: Bank and financial institutions offer loans to help individuals to purchase vehicles, with the car acting as collateral.

Advantages:

- Lower interest rates due to the presence of collateral

- Longer repayment terms, often extending up to 30 years.

Disadvantages:

- Risk of losing the asset if the borrower defaults.

2. Unsecured Loans

Unsecured loans are loans that do not require any collateral. The lender provides the loan based on the borrower's creditworthiness, income and other factors. These loans typically carry higher interest rates due to the increased risk to the lender.

Examples:

- **Personal loan**: Personal loans are unsecured loans that can be used for any purpose, including medical expenses, travel or home improvement.

- **Credit Card Loans**: Credit cards allow borrower to access credit which they can repay in monthly installments or all at once

Advantages:

- No collateral is required.

- Faster approval and disbursement.

Disadvantages:

- Higher interest rates.

- Strict eligibility criteria, such as a good credit score.

3. Business Loans

Business loans are provided to businesses to help them fund various operations, such as expansion, working capital or buying equipment. These loans can be secured or unsecured depending on the financial health of the business and its assets.

Examples:

- **Small Business Loans**: The Indian government has launched several schemes like the MUDRA (Micro Units Development and Refinancing Agency) loan to help small businesses access funds.

- **Working Capital Loans**: These loans provide businesses with the funds they need for daily operational expensed like salaries, rent and inventory.

Advantages:

- Helps businesses to grow and manage their operations.

- Tax benefits in some cases.

Disadvantages:

- Risk of default if the business fails to generate enough revenue.

4. Education Loans

Education loans are designed to help individuals pursue higher education by funding their tuition fees, books, and other related expenses. These loans are often offered by public and private banks with lower interest rates and flexible repayment options.

Advantages:

- Low interest rates, especially for government backed loans.

- Grace period after course completion before starting repayment.

Disadvantages:

- The borrower may face difficulty in repaying if they do not secure employment immediately after completing their studies.

5. Gold Loans

Gold loans are loans where the borrower pledges their gold jewelry as collateral. Gold loan are popular in India because of the cultural significance of gold and ease of obtaining them.

Advantages:

- Quick disbursal of funds.

- Lower interest rates compared to unsecured loans.

Disadvantages:

- Risk of losing the gold if the loan is not repaid

6. Agriculture Loans

Agriculture loans are designed to meet the financial needs of farmers. These loans help them to purchase seeds, equipment or fertilizers and manage other aspects of farming.

Example:

- **Kisan Credit Cards (KCC)**: This scheme, offered b banks in India provides farmers with access to working capital for agriculture purposes.

Advantages:

- Lower interest rates and flexible repayment terms.

- Government support in case of natural calamities or crop failure.

Disadvantages:

- Farmers often facing difficulties in repaying loans due to factors like unpredictable weather condition.

Who Should Take a Loan and why?

Loans are beneficial for people who need financial support to achieve specific goals, provided they have the capacity to repay the loan. Below are examples of who might need a loan and why:

1. Homebuyers

Homebuyers who cannot afford to purchase property upfront often take out home loans to buy a house. A home loan allows them to repay the amount in installments over a long period (15-30 years) making home ownership accessible.

2. Students

Students who need funds to pursue higher education, especially in institutions where the fees are high, often turn to student loans. These loans help them manage tuition fees, living expenses and other related costs.

3. Business Owners

Entrepreneurs and business owners may need loans to fund their business operations, expand their enterprises or purchase equipment. Business loans can provide the necessary capital to ensure growth and sustainability.

4.   Individuals Facing Emergency Situations

Sometimes people may face urgent financial needs due to medical emergencies, weddings or other unforeseen circumstances. Personal loans can help them to manage such situations without depleting their savings.

Points to Keep in Mind While Taking Loans

1.   **Understand the Loan terms:** Always read the fine print. Understand the interest rate, repayment schedule and any associated fees before taking out a loan.

2.   **Evaluate your Repayment Capacity**: Ensure that you can comfortably repay the loan amount without straining your finances. It's important to have a clear understanding of your income and expenses.

3.   **Choose the Right Loan Type**: Different loans serve different purposes. Choose a loan that aligns with your needs – whether it's home loan, personal loan or educational loan.

4.   **Check the Interest Rate**: Compare interest rates from different lenders to find the most affordable loan. Even a small difference in the interest rate can significantly affect the total cost of the loan over time.

5.   **Know the Impact on your Credit Score**: Timely repayment of loans improves your credit card score, while late payments can hurt it. Always ensure that you make payment on time.

6. **Avoid Over borrowing**: Only borrow what you can afford to repay. Taking excessive loans may lead to debt accumulation and financial strain.

Loans play a crucial role in the economy, providing individuals and business with the financial resources needed to fulfill their goals. However, borrowing should always be done cautiously. It is essential to understand the different types of loan evaluate repayment capacity and compare lenders before making a decision. Taking loans without proper consideration and lead to financial distress. Responsible borrowing is key to leveraging loans effectively to achieve financial objectives without falling into a debt trap.

KEY TAKE AWAY

- Understand the interest rates and fees of loans

- Ensure whether the loan has a fixed or variable interest rates

- Understand the risks if you default on payment

- Your home loan amount shouldn't be more than 4 to 5 times of your annual income

- Your car loan amount should not exceed to your annual income

GOLD

"Gold is the currency of rich and the poor alike"

The history of gold as it pertains to finance is rich, deeply intertwined with the development of human civilization and highly influential in shaping the modern financial system. As one of the oldest and most stable forms of money, gold has earned the title of "God's Money" due to durability, scarcity and universal acceptance.

1. The History of Gold in Finance

Gold's use as money dates back to the ancient civilizations. It has been valued for thousands of years, first as a symbol of wealth and power and later as a medium of exchange. The earliest recorded use of gold as currency occurred around 600 BCE in Lydia, a kingdom in what is now modern day Turkey. The Lydians minted the first coins made of electrum a naturally occurring alloy of gold and silver. This marked the beginning of a long relationship between gold and money.

Gold intrinsic qualities made it in ideal medium for trade and investment. It is durable, doesn't corrode or tarnish and can be divided into smaller units without losing value. Gold was used for coins, jewelry and as a store of value. The ancient Egyptians, Greeks and Romans all recognized the importance of Gold. The Romans in particular used gold extensively in coinage which helps establish it as a standard currency throughout their empire.

In the middle Ages, gold continued to serve as symbol of wealth. During this period the use of gold coins spread across Europe and the Middle East. The Islamic Empire for instance issued the gold Dinar, which became a widely accepted country.

In the 17th and 18th centuries, the European economies were significantly bolstered by the discovery of Gold in Americas, particularly during the Spanish conquest in the New Word. Gold and Silver were the foundations of the early international trade systems. As trade expanded, so did the demand for gold as a reliable store of value and a medium of exchange.

The 19th century saw the formalization of the gold standards, where nations fixed the value of their currencies to a certain quantity of gold. This practice provided stability to the international markets. The gold standard becomes the backbone of the global financial system, facilitating trade and limiting inflation.

The Bretton Woods system, established after World War-II, continued the tradition of linking currencies to gold, However in 1971 President Richard Nixon took the United State off the gold standard effectively ending the Bretton Woods agreement. This move shifted the global financial system from being commodity based to fiat money systems where the value of currency is not backed by physical commodities but by government trust.

Despite the move to fiat currencies, gold has retained its role as a hedge against inflation and economic uncertainty. It is still widely seen as a store of value particularly during times of financial crises when people seek safe havens for their wealth.

2. Why Gold is Called "God's Money"

Gold has earned the title "God's Money" for several reasons. This nickname is often used to emphasis the almost divine qualities attributed to gold throughout hyman history. Its unique properties, rarity and cultural significance all contribute to this reverence.

- **Scarcity and Durability:** Gold is relatively rare in the earth's crust, which has made it valuable for millennia. It doesn't corrode, rust, or tarnish, making it one of the most durable materials known to man. Because of this gold has withstood the test of time maintaining its value and appeal across centuries and civilizations

- **Intrinsic Value**: Unlike paper money which can be printed in unlimited quantities, the supply of gold is constraint by nature. This inherent scarcity has made it is a symbol of wealth that cannot be inflated to manipulated in the same way as fiat currencies.

- **Cultural and Religious Significance:** Throughout History, gold has held religious and cultural significance in many societies. It has been associated with deities and the divine, often symbolizing purity wealth and eternity. In many religions gold is seen as a representation of divine power and favor. In Christianity for example the Three Wise Men brought gold as a gift to the infant Jesus, further embedding gold's divine associations in western culture.

- **Universal Acceptance:** Gold's appeal spans cultures, Continents and time periods. It has been universally accepted as store of value and a form of walth. This universal acceptance, coupled with its durability, rarity and beauty that is why it has been revered and cherished throughout history.

3. Why You Should Buy Physical Gold?

Gold is considered a safe haven for investors, particularly in times of economic uncertainty. Here are several reasons why buying physical gold is a prudent financial decision:

- **Hedge against Inflation and Currency Devaluation**: Gold is often considered a hedge against inflation because its value tends to rise when the purchasing power of falls. In times of economic uncertainty, central banks may print more money, leading to inflation and currency devaluation. Gold however retains its intrinsic value, making it an effective way to preserve wealth.

- **Store of Value:** Physical gold acts as a store of value that is independent of the performance of any single currency or financial market. Unlike stocks or bonds, which can be subject to volatility, gold's value tends to remain stable over time. This makes it a reliable asset for long term wealth.

- **Portfolio Diversification:** Adding physical gold to your investment portfolio can help diversify your holdings. Because gold typically moves in the opposite direction to riskier assets, reducing the overall volatility of your portfolio.

- **Tangible Asset:** Unlike digital assets or paper investments, physical gold is a tangible asset that you can hold in your hands. This provides a sense of security and control, particularly in times of financial instability of digital when people may question the stability of digital or fiat currencies.

- **No Counterparty Risk:** Physical gold is free from the counterparty risk that affects other investments. For instance stocks and bonds are tied to the financial health of corporations or governments and there is always the risk that the issuer could default. Physical gold on the other hand is not reliant on any third party.

- **Global Liquidity:** Gold is universally recognized which means it can be sold or exchanged anywhere in the world. Whether you're in the United States, Europe, Asia, or Africa, physical gold can be easily traded for cash or used as collateral for loans.

- **Wealth Preservation Across Generation:** Physical gold can be passed down through generations, making it a reliable asset for wealth preservation and inheritance planning. It is often seen as a generational store of value, ensuring that wealth is preserved even in times of political instability.

4. How Much Physical Gold Should You Buy?

The amount of physical gold you should purchase depends on several factors, including your financial goals, risk tolerance, and overall portfolio diversification strategy. Here are some general guidelines:

- **Diversification Strategy:** While gold is a great asset for diversifying your portfolio, it should not constitute the majority of your wealth. Financial experts recommend allocating between 5% to 10% of your portfolio to gold, though this can vary based on your personal financial situation and outlook on the economy.

- **Risk Tolerance:** If you are risk averse or concerned about economic instability, you might want to allocate a higher percentage of your wealth to gold. Conversely if you have a higher risk tolerance a lower allocation might be appropriate.

- **Long Term wealth Preservation:** If your primary goal is wealth preservation rather than short-term gains, then investing in physical gold over time can be sound strategy. It may be wise to gradually accumulate gold through regular purchases, building your holding over time.

- **Economic Outlook**: If you anticipate inflation, currency devaluation, or economic downturns, it may be prudent to increase your gold holdings. However if you expect the economy to remain stable and thriving, you might not to prioritize gold as much in your strategy.

5. **Pros and Cons of Purchasing Gold**

Pros:

- **Tangible and Portable:** Physical gold is tangible and easy to store. It provides a sense of security and can be transported or stored privately, away from the digital system that can be vulnerable to hacking or system failures.

- **Global Acceptance:** Gold is universally recognized as a store of value and can be easily liquidated in markets across the world.

- **No Counterparty Risk:** Unlike stocks or bonds, physical gold carries no counterparty risk. You don't have to rely on third parties, such as banks or government to back your investment.

- **Wealth Preservation:** Gold is stable store of value over long periods, making it ideal for preserving wealth during times of financial instability or market downturns.

- **Inflation edge:** Gold has historically been a strong hedge against inflation as its value often rises when the purchasing power of fiat currencies falls.

Cons:

- **Storage and security:** Physical gold requires secure storage such as a safe or vault. This can incur additional costs and potential costs and potential risks related to theft or loss.

- **Liquidity:** While gold is liquid, selling physical gold might not be as straightforward or fast as selling digital assets or stocks especially if you are selling in small quantities.

- **No Passive income**: Unlike stocks or bonds, physical gold does not generate dividends or interest. It simply sits as a store of value and its potential returns depend on price appreciation over time.

- **Premium and Fees**: When purchasing physical gold often pay a premium above the spot price particularly for coins or bars. Additionally you may face transaction fees and storage costs which can eat into your profits.

- **Market Volatility:** While gold is a stable asset over the long term, its short-term price can still be volatile. Economic events, changes in interest rates and shifts in investor sentiment can cause gold prices to fluctuate.

By buying physical gold individual can protect their wealth against inflation, economic instability and market volatility. However like any investments purchasing physical gold comes with its own set of advantages and disadvantages. Understanding these factors and how gold fits into your overall investment strategy.

KEY TAKE AWAY

- Gold has long term store of value

- Gold helps in diversify your portfolio

- Gold often seen as a hedge against inflation

- Gold has various investment options (coin, bars, jewelry, gold ETFs etc)

- Gold provides long term wealth preservation

Real Estate

"Don't wait to buy real estate. Buy real estate and wait"

-- T. Harv Eker

Real estate is one of the most significant sectors of any economy, and India's real estate market is no exception. Real estate investments in India have been historically considered a reliable option for wealth creation. However, like any investment it requires careful consideration of various factors including the financial dynamics of the market, economic conditions and individual risk tolerance.

1. Understanding the Real Estate Market in India

The Indian real estate market consists of various segments including residential, commercial and the retail properties as well as land. The market is driven by numerous factors such as urbanization, population growth, economic development, interest rates, government policies and changing consumer preferences. The real estate sector in India is a significant contributor to the country's GDP, creating millions of job and providing substantial returns to investors. There are following market segments:

- **Residential Real Estate:** This segment deals with properties intended for residential purposes, such as apartment, houses and condominiums. The demand for residential real estate is primarily driven by population growth, urbanization, increasing disposable incomes and government incentives like affordable housing scheme.

- **Commercial Real Estate:** This involves properties used for business purposes, including office spaces, shopping centers, hotels and industrial properties. The demand for commercial real estate is often influenced by the state of the economy, business growth and foreign direct investment (FDI).

- **Retail Real Estate:** This is a subset of commercial real estate that includes retail spaces like malls and stores. With the rise of online shopping, the retail real estate segment has seen fluctuations, though it remains crucial in urban markets.

- **Industrial Real Estate:** This category focuses on manufacturing units, warehouse and distribution centers. As e-commerce and logistics industries grow, the demand for industrial real estate is also on the rise in India.

2. Why invest in Real Estate in India?

India's real estate market is attractive to both domestic and international investors due to several factors:

- **Economic Growth:** India is one of the world's fastest-growing major economies, and the government's emphasis on infrastructure development, urbanization and industrialization boosts demand for real estate across the country.

- **Population Growth**: With over 1.4 billion people, India is the second-most populate country in the world. A significant portion of this population is young, leading to increased demand for housing and commercial spaces especially in urban areas.

- **Urbanization:** India is witnessing rapid urbanization with more people moving to cities for job opportunities and better living standards. The growing urban population translates into higher demand for residential and commercial real estate in metropolitan cities.

- **Investment Diversification:** Real estate is a relatively stable asset class compared to stocks and bonds. Investors can diversify their portfolio by adding real estate, reducing overall risk and enhancing long-term returns.

- **High Returns and Capital Appreciation:** Over the long term in India has provided attractive returns, particularly in major cities like Mumbai, Delhi, Bangalore and Pune. Additionally property prices tend to appreciate over time due to limited supply, increasing demand and infrastructure developments.

- **Rental Income:** For investors looking for a steady income stream, rental properties can provide monthly or quarterly rental income. India's large population and growing middle class ensure there is demand for both residential and commercial properties.

- **Tax Benefits:** Investors in Indian real estate can take advantage of tax deduction on home loan interest and principal repayment.

3. How Much Should One Invest in Real Estate?

Deciding how much to invest in real estate depends on various factors, such as one's financial goals, risk tolerance, current financial situation and the type of real estate investment. Here are the key considerations:

- **Investment Horizon:** Real estate investing generally require a long-term commitment. If your goal is to accumulate wealth over several years, investing a larger proportion of your savings in real estate may be appropriate. However if you are looking for short-term gains, real estate may not be the best investment.

- **Diversification:** Financial advisors typically recommend diversification across asset classes to reduce risk. If you have significant investments in equities or fixed-income instruments, allocating 20% to 30% of your portfolio to real estate might offer an optimal balance between risk and return.

- **Financial Capacity:** The amount you can invest in real estate should be aligned with your financial capacity. You should never over-leverage or stretch your finance to invest in real estate. A good rule of thumb is to invest in real estate only if you can comfortably afford the down payment and manage the subsequent mortgage payments and property-related expenses.

- **Risk Tolerance:** Real estate is not a risk free investment and the market can be volatile, especially in urban areas. Consider your risk tolerance and your ability to handle market fluctuation before making any investment. If you prefer low-risk investments consider investing in REITs (Real Estate Investment Trust) which provide exposure to real estate markets without the direct ownership risks.

- **Location and Market condition**: The amount you should invest also depends on the location of property. Major cities like Delhi, Mumbai, Hyderabad have higher property prices but they also tend to provide higher returns due to their booming economies and high demand for real estate. However smaller towns or emerging cities may offer lower entry prices and higher potential for growth in the long term.

4. Points to Keep in Mind while Investing in Real Estate

India's real estate market is attractive to both domestic and international investors due to several factors:

1. Research the market Thoroughly

Before investing in real estate, it's crucial to conduct through research on the property market, including price trends, demand and supply dynamics, location potential and upcoming developments. Research will give you insights into whether the area is poised for growth or if it's already saturated.

- **Price Trends:** Understand historical price movements and analyze whether property prices are expected to rise or fall the short and long term.

- **Infrastructure Development:** Look for properties near key infrastructure projects such as highways, metro stations and airport as these can drive up property values.

2. Location is the Key

In real estate, location is paramount. The property's location will determine not to only its value but its future appreciation potential. Factors to consider include:

- Proximity is essential service such as school, hospital and shopping centers.

- Accessibility to public transportation.

- Future urban development in the area which could increase the property's value over time.

3. Legal Due Diligence

Ensure that the property you are considering is legally sound. This involves verifying the ownership, title deed and zoning regulations. It's essential to check if the property has clear titles and no pending legal disputes.

Properties with unclear ownership or land use issues cal lead to significant complications.

- **Verify Land title:** Ensure the property title is clear and not subject to and disputes.

- **Encumbrance Certificate:** This document certifies that the property is free of legal dues and mortgages.

4. Financing options

Real estate investments usually involve significant capital outlay and most investors will need financing. In India, several banks and financial institution offers home loans with varying interest rate, loan tenures, and repayment options. It is crucial to compare various lenders before selecting the one that suits your financial situation.

- **Loan to Value (LTV) Ratio**: Typically, a banks offer loans upto 80% of the property value, meaning the buyers needs to contribute the remaining 20% as a down payment.

- **Interest Rates:** Choose a loan with competitive interest rates to reduce the overall cost of your investment.

5. Property Management

Managing a property involves maintenance, talent management, rent collection and dealing with legalities. If you are investing in rental properties, ensure that you have a property manager or a real estate agent who can handle these tasks efficiently.

Professional property management services can help maximize rental income and reduce vacancy periods.

6. Consider Future Liquidity

Real estate is not a liquid asset. Selling property can take time and you may not always achieve the desired price especially in a market downturn.

Hence its important to have sufficient liquidity in your portfolio for emergencies or short-term financial needs. You should not invest all your savings in real estate as it may lead to liquidity constraint.

7. Tax Implication

While real estate investment offers various tax benefits, there are also taxes and charges associated with owning property in India. Investors must be aware of the applicable stamp duty, property tax, capital gain tax and income tax on rental income.

Understanding these taxes and structuring your investment accordingly can help optimize your returns

- **Stamp Duty:** This is one-time tax paid on the transfer of property ownerships. Rates vary by state.

- **Capital Gains Tax:** If you sell a property for more than you purchased it, you will need to pay capital gains tax. The rate depends on the holding period (long term or short term).

- **Rental Income Tax:** Income earned from renting out property is taxable under income tax laws.

8. What's better: owning a home or renting one?

Whether it's better to own a house or live on rent depends on your personal goals, financial situation and lifestyle preferences. Here are a few points to consider:

Advantage of Owning a House:

- **Building Equity**: When you own a house you're building equity over time as the property value may appreciate and your mortgage balance decreases.

- **Stability:** Homeownership can provide more stability and security as you're not subject to rent hikes or eviction.

- **Freedom:** You have the freedom to modify and renovate the property as you wish, without needing landlord approval.

- **Long Term Investment:** Real estate is often seen as good long-term investment if the property value appreciates over time.

- **Asset Transfer:** The emotion of passing down an asset transfer to the next generation is a cherished legacy for every parent. Through careful planning, a parent ensures smooth transfer of assets to benefit the next generation.

Advantage of Renting:

- **Flexibility:** Renting provide flexibility is you plan on moving frequently for work, lifestyle or personal reasons.

- **Low initial costs:** Renting typically requires less upfront money.

- **No maintenance costs:** Renters don't need to worry about repairs, maintenance or property taxes which can be costly for homeowners.

- **Financial Risk:** Renting doesn't carry same financial risks as homeowners (e.g. market fluctuations, property damage)

Real estate investment in India offers lucrative opportunities for investors looking for capital appreciation, regular income and long-term growth.

The growing economy, urbanization and favorable government policies have made the Indian real estate market an attractive destination for investors. However like any investment it requires due diligence, proper research and careful planning. By understanding the financial dynamics of the market, assessing your financial capacity and keeping in mind key factors like location, legal issues and property management, you can make sound real estate investment decision that align with your financial goal.

KEY TAKE AWAY

- Real estate can provide consistent rental income

- Property values often increase over time

- Real estate provide hedge against inflation

- Real estate has high appreciation potential

- Real estate gives emotion of pride in building long-term wealth and pass it on to your new generation

Mutual Funds

"Don't put all your eggs in one basket"

- Warren Buffett

A mutual fund is a type of investment vehicle that pools money from multiple investors to invest in a diversified portfolio of stocks, bonds or other securities. The fund is managed by professional fund managers who make investment decisions on behalf of the investors based on the fund objectives.

In simple terms, a mutual fund allows individual investors to combine their money with others to invest in a variety of assets. Each investor to combine their money with others to invest in a variety of assets. Each investor own shares in the mutual fund, which represent a portion of the holding in the fund's portfolio. The value of these shares fluctuates with the performance of the underlying assets and investors can buy or sell shares in the fund.

Global History of Mutual Funds

1. Early Beginnings: The concept of Pooling Resources

The roots of mutual funds can be traced back to the concept of pooling resources in various forms of communal investing. In the 18th century, the Dutch-developed the first modern mutual fund-like structure. The **Dutch East India**

Company in the 1600s allow investors to pool money for large trade ventures, and their model provided the foundation for later developments in mutual fund structure.

However the first true mutual fund is often credited to the creation of the **Investment Company of America** in the United States in 1924. This fund allowed small investors to pool their resources in a manner that enabled them to invest in a diversified portfolio of stocks, could now benefit from collective investing.

2. Early 20th Century: The Birth of the Modern Mutual Fund

The early 20th century saw the formalization of the mutual fund industry in several countries. In the United States, the first investment company, The Masssachusetts Investors Trust (MIT), was established in 1924 by **Thomas Rowe Price**, avisionary in the field of investment, Price is considered one of the pioneers of mutual fund as he introduced the concept of professional management to mutual funds, allowing individuals to invest in a diversified portfolio under the guidance of a fund manager.

Mutual fund gained further Traction as the concept of **pooling investor capital** to reduce risk and enhance returns became more widely accepted. At this point, investment companies began offering a wide range of funds, including funds invested in bonds, Stocks and real estate. The Securities and Exchange Commission (SEC), established in 1934 in the U.S, began to regulate the industry to ensure transparency and protect investors.

3. Mid-20th Century: Growth and Popularization

The mutual funds industry saw significant growth post-World War II. In the 1950s, and 1960s, the economy of the United States grew rapidly, spurring investment in the stock market. During this period, mutual funds became more popular among retail investors as they provided an easy entry point for individuals who lacked the time or expertise to manage their own portfolios.

The 1950s also saw the established of one of the most successful and influential investment firms in the mutual fund space: **Fidelity Investment.** In1946, Edward C. Jonson II took control of fidelity introduced the concept of actively managed mutual funds, where fund managers made decisions based on market trends and research, rather than simply following an index.

As the financial market expanded, more sophisticated and diversified types of mutual funds emerged, such as Index Funds, which aimed to mirror the performance of a market index like the S&P 500. This innovation was a major step toward passive investing sought to match market returns rather than beat them.

4. Late 20th Century: The Rise in Index Funds and Globalization

The 1970s and 1980s witnessed another critical milestone in the development of mutual funds: the introduction of **Index Funds.** In 1975, Jack Bogle, founder of the **Vanguard Group,** launched the first index fund, the First Index

Investment Trust, which sought to replicate the performance of the S&P 500 index. The launch of index funds marked a paradigm shift in investment strategies, as they were cheaper to manage and aimed to provide steady returns in line with overall market performance.

During this time, Mutual funds became increasingly popular in countries outside the United States. The United Kingdom and European markets began to embrace the mutual fund model, and the growing wealth in emerging economies led to the introduction of mutual funds in countries like Japan, Brazil and South Korea.

5. 21st Century: Diversification and Technological Integration

The 21st century has brought both challenges and opportunities to the mutual fund industry, **The 2008 Global Financial Crisis** (GFC) tested the resilience of mutual funds, as many funds suffered significant losses. The GFC prompted regulatory reforms and an increased focus on risk management and transparency. It also sparked greater demand for alternative investment such as hedge funds and private equity funds.

In the post GFC era, mutual fund have continued to evolve with the rise of **Exchange Traded Funds** (ETFs), which combine features of mutual funds and individual stocks, offering investors greater liquidity and lower costs. ETFs have become a significant alternative to traditional mutual funds due to their flexibility and cost- effectiveness.

Simultaneously, technology innovations, such as the rise of robo-advisors and digital platforms, have democratized investing, allowing retail investors to access mutual fund in an easy and affordable manner. These platforms use algorithms to create diversified portfolios for individual investors based on their risk profiles, making mutual fund investing accessible to a broader demographic.

Today, mutual funds are a multi-trillion-dollar industry globally, offering a wide range of investment options for individual and institutional investors. These funds cater to various investment strategies, including equity funds, bond funds, sector funds, international funds and **sustainable or socially responsible funds**.

History of Mutual Funds in India

1. Pre-Independence Period: Beginnings of Collective Investments

India's mutual fund industry has its roots in the early 20th century, through it was initially slow to develop. The first recorded mutual fund in India was **The Indian Investment Trust Ltd,** established in 1860. However, this was very small entity, and it was more of a collective investment pool for affluent Indian investors.

India's modern mutual fund industry began to take shape after the country gained independence in 1947. Post-Independence, India's economy was primarily agrarian and closed off from global financial markets. The financial sector in India was developed, and there was limited exposure to investment product like mutual funds.

2. 1960s-1970s: The Birth of Public Sector Mutual Funds

The Indian mutual fund industry took a significant step forward in the 1960s when the **Unit Trust of India (UTI)** was established in 1963 by an ACT of Parliament. UTI was created with the goal of mobilizing savings from small investors in government securities and other instruments. UTI became a prominent player in the Indian mutual fund a prominent player in the Indian mutual fund space for several decades and was backed by the Indian government.

However, It was the **nationalization of banks** in 1969 and the establishment of **Life Insurance Corporation of India (LIC)** in 1656 that opened up opportunities for the public to invest in government- backed financial products. Despite these developments, the mutual fund market was not fully established until much later.

3. 1980s-1990s: Liberalization and Entry of Private Players

The real turning point for India's mutual fund industry came in the early 1990s, during the era of economic liberalization. In 1991, under **Finance Minister Manmohan Singh,** India opened up its economy and began to integrate with global markets. This period also saw the establishments of the **Securities and Exchange Board of India (SEBI)** in

1992, which provided a regulatory framework for financial markets.

In 1993 the Indian mutual fund industry saw the entry of private players, starting with the launch of private players, starting with the launch of **ICICI Mutual Fund**.

The LIC Mutual Fund follows on 1994, and the several other private-sector mutual funds were established thereafter. These developments marked a significant shift in the mutual fund landscape, as investors now had more options and greater diversification in the funds they could choose from.

4. 2000s: Growth and Regulation

In the early 2000s, the Indian mutual fund industry experience exponential growth. By the turn of the century, the number of mutual funds had increased and SEBI had introduced a comprehensive set of regulations to ensure transparency, investor protection and the smooth functioning of the industry. Mutual funds, once considered an investment product for the affluent, began to gain popularity among the middle class.

During this period, **Systematic Investment Plans (SIPs)** became a popular investment route for small investors a popular investment route for small investors. SIPs allowed investors to invest fixed amount of money into a mutual fund at a regular intervals to invest in the stock market while mitigating the risks of market volatility.

The introduction of **New Fund Offers (NFOs)** further contributed to the growth of the sector and asset under management (AUM) surged. BY 2005, mutual funds had become an integral part of the Indian investments landscape, with equity funds emerging as the most popular investment option among Indian investors.

5. 2010s: Mutual Funds and the Retail Investor

The 2010s marked a period of widespread awareness about mutual funds in India. Digital platforms, mobile apps and online investing grew rapidly, giving retail investors easy access to mutual fund investments. The growth of **exchange-traded funds (ETFs)** and the rise of sustainable investing reflected changing investors preferences.

The **Mutual Fund Sahi Hai** campaign, launched by the Indian Mutual Fund Industry in 2015, was a key driver in improving awareness about the benefits of mutual fund investments among India retail investors. SEBI also implemented several reforms, such as introducing a Direct Plan for mutual funds, which eliminated commission fees and allowed investors to invest directly in mutual funds.

The expansion of the mutual fund industry was also fueled b the introduction of Liquid Funds, Debt Funds and Hybrid Funds which provided options for different risks profiles and investment needs.

6. 2020s: Current Trends and Future Prospects

As of the 2020s, the mutual fund industry in India has reached new heights. Assets under management have crossed significant milestones and mutual funds have become one of the most preferred investment vehicles for retail investors. The industry continues to see the growth of SIPs, index funds and ETFs, driven by investors' desire for long-term wealth creation.

India's mutual fund market has evolved to become more competitive, with a mix of private-sector and international players offering a range of products. The increased focus on financial literacy, the growth of digital economy and regulatory oversight has all contributed to the maturation of the industry.

The future of mutual funds in India appears promising, driven by the increasing participation of the middle-class investor, the growth of the digital economy and regulatory support from SEBI. As more Indian investors realize the benefits of investing in mutual funds, the industry will evolve with innovative products and enhanced investor services.

What is Large Cap, Mid Cap and Cap Small Funds?

In mutual funds, the term small-cap, Mid cap and Large cap refers to the market capitalization (Market Cap) of the companies in which the fund invests. Market capitalization is the total value of a company's outstanding shares of stock, calculated by multiplying the current share price by the total number of shares. These classifications are primarily based on the size of the companies and they offer different risk and return profiles. The value of these categories in terms of market cap is typically defined by the market regulations and change over time due to market fluctuations.

In the context of India, here is how the different categories are generally defined:

1. Large-Cap Funds

Large-cap funds invest primarily in large-cap companies, which are biggest and most well-established companies in the market. These companies are typically well-established with a history of stable performance. They are also less volatile compared to smaller companies.

Market Cap Range for Large- Cap Companies

- Companies with a market capitalization above ₹ 20,000 crore are typically considered large-cap companies.

2. Mid-Cap Funds

Mid-cap funds in mid-cap companies, which are medium-sized companies that are generally in the growth phase. These companies have the potential to grow rapidly, but they come with a higher level of risk compared to large-cap companies.

Market Cap Range for Large- Cap Companies

- Companies with a market capitalization between ₹ 5,000 crore and ₹ 20,000 crore are classified as mid-cap companies.

3. Small-Cap Funds

Small-cap funds invest in small-cap companies, which are relatively newer or smaller companies with a lower market capitalization. These companies offer higher growth potential but are often riskier and more volatile compared to mid-cap or large-cap companies

Market Cap Range for Large- Cap Companies

- Companies with a market capitalization less than ₹ 5,000 crore are considered small-cap companies.

Types of Mutual Funds and How They work

Mutual fund has become one of the most popular investment options for individuals in India due to their ability to pool investments and provide diversification. In mutual fund, investors contribute money to a common pool managed by professional fund managers, who allocate the capital into various financial instruments such as equities, bonds and other assets. Depending on the type of mutual fund, the investment focus and risk exposure can vary significantly.

In India mutual funds are regulated by the Securities and Exchange Board of India (SEBI) to ensure transparency, fair practices and investors protection. Here we will explores the various types of mutual funds available in India, explaining their investment objectives, asset allocation and the way they operate. The main types of mutual funds in India are equity funds, debt funds, hybrid funds, index funds, sectoral funds, exchange traded funds (ETFs) and thematic funds.

1. Equity Mutual Funds

Equity mutual funds primarily invest in stocks of equities, making them high-risk, high-reward investments. These funds aim to generate returns by capital appreciation in the stock market. Equity funds are suitable for long-term investors who have a higher risk tolerance and seek higher returns over time.

How Does an Equity Mutual Fund Work?

- **Investment focus:** The fund manager invests more than 60% of its total assets in the equity shared of different companies. The balance amount can be invested in money market instrument or debt securities as per the investment objectives of the scheme.

- **Risk and Return:** Since equities are volatile, equity funds can experience high fluctuation in value. However, over the long term, they tend to provide higher returns than other asset classes like debt.

Types of Equity Funds:

- **Large-cap Funds:** These funds invest in companies with large market capitalization. (Typically those are part if major indices like the NIFTY 50 or Sensex) They are considered safer or more stable.

- **Mid-cap Funds**: These funds invest in mid-sized companies, which are typically more volatile but have higher growth potential.

- **Small-cap Funds:** These funds invest in smaller companies with high growth potential but are subject to greater volatility and risk.

- **Sector or Thematic Funds:** These funds invest in specific sectors or themes, such as technology, infrastructure or healthcare which means they are subject to the performance of that sector.

- **Diversify Equity Funds:** These funds invest across a wide range of stocks and sectors, providing broad exposure to the equity markets.

2. Debt Mutual Funds

Debt mutual funds invest in fixed-income securities such as bonds, government securities, corporate bonds and money market instruments.

The primary objective of these funds is to provide regular income with lower risk than equity funds. Debt funds are suitable for conservatives' investors or those seeking stable returns with lower risk.

How Does Debt Mutual Fund Work?

- **Investment focus:** Debt funds invest in a range of debt instruments such as government bonds, corporate bonds, commercial papers, treasury bills and other fixed-income securities. The type of debt instrument depends on the fund's objective.

- **Risk and Return:** Debt fund carry lower risk than equity funds, but their returns are also typically lower. The returns in debt funds are affected by factors like interest rates, credit risk and the maturity of the underlying bonds.

Types of Debt Funds:

- **Liquid Funds:** These funds invest in short-term instrument with a maturity of up to 91 days. They are considered the safest among debt funds and are used for parking short-term surplus funds.

- **Short terms Funds:** These funds invest in securities with a maturity period of 1 to 3 years. They offer higher returns than liquid funds but come slightly more risk.

- **Income Funds:** These funds invest in ling-term debt instruments with a higher yield. They have a longer duration and are affected by changes in interest rates.

- **Gilt Funds:** These funds invest in government securities, which are considered risk free. They are ideal for conservative investors looking for low-risk stable returns.

- **Credit Risk Funds**: These funds focus on bonds and securities issued by companies with lower credit ratings. They offer higher returns but come with a higher risk of default.

3. Hybrid Mutual Funds

Hybrid mutual funds combine investments in both equities and debt instruments, thus providing a balance of risk and return. The primary goal of hybrid funds is to offer through equity exposure while ensuring some stability through debt investments. These funds are suited for investors who want diversification without taking on the risks of a pure equity fund.

How Does Hybrid Mutual Fund Work?

- **Investment focus:** Hybrid funds typically invest in both stocks and fixed-income securities, with the allocation depending on the fund's objective. For example, a balanced fund might have a 60% allocation to equities and 40% to debt, while other hybrid funds might have different combinations.

- **Risk and Return:** Hybrid funds offer moderate risk and moderate returns. The equity portion provides growth potential, while the debt portion adds stability and income.

Types of Hybrid Funds:

- **Balanced Funds:** These funds aim for a balance between growth (through equity investment) and income (through debt investments). They typically have a 60:40 or 70:30 equity-to-debt ratio.

- **Aggressive Hybrid Funds:** These funds have a higher allocation to equities (usually 65% to 80%) and focus more on growth, but with some stability provided by debt investments.

- **Conservative Hybrid Funds:** These funds have a higher allocation to debt instruments (usually 60% to 70%) and a smaller portion invested in equities. They are suited for risk averse investors who still want some exposure to the stock market.

- **Dynamic Asset Allocation Funds:** These funds change the equity and debt allocation based on market conditions. The fund manager decides the allocation depending on market outlook, making them more flexible.

4.   Index Mutual Funds

Index funds are a type of mutual funds that aim to replicate the performance of a particular market index, such as the NIFTY 50 or the Sensex. Instead of actively managing the portfolio, the fund manager invests in the same stocks that are part of the index, maintaining the same weightage.

How Does Index Mutual Fund Work?

- **Investment focus:** The primary focus of index funds is to match the performance of a specific index. For instance, Nifty 50 index fund will invest in the 50 companies that are part of the Nifty 50 Index.

- **Risk and Return:** Since index funds invest in the stocks that constitute the index, their returns are tied directly to the performance of that index. The risk is lower compared to actively managed equity funds because there is less chance of underperformance or higher volatility. Index funds are passive in nature, meaning they have lower management fees than actively managed funds.

Types of Index Funds:

- **Nifty 50 Index Funds:** These funds replicate the performance of the Nifty 50 index, which consists of 50 large-cap companies listed on the National Stock Exchange (NSE) of India. These are among the most popular index funds in india.

- **Sensex Index funds:** These funds track the BSE Sensex, which includes 30 large-cap companies listed on the Bombay stock Exchange (BSE). Similar to Nifty 50 funds, these aim to mirror the performance of the sensex index.

- **Nifty Next 50 Index Funds:** These funds track the Nifty next 50 index, which includes the next 50 companies after the Nifty 50, offering exposure to mid cap stocks.

- **Bank Nifty Index Funds:** These funds replicate the performance of the Nifty Bank Index, which comprises 12 of the most liquid and large banking stocks in India. They are suitable for those looking to invest specifically in the banking sector.

- **Nifty 500 Index Funds:** Theses funds track the Nifty 500 index, which include 500 companies across large, mid and small-cap categories, giving investors broad market exposure.

- **International Index Funds:** These funds, track global indices like the S&P 500, allowing Indian investors to gain exposure to international markets,

Examples include funds tracking the S&P 500 such as the Nippon india S7P 500 index fund.

- **ESG (Environment, Social, and Governance) Index Funds:** These funds invest in companies that meet specific environmental, social and governance criteria. They track indices such as the Nifty 100 ESG index

Why One should Invest in Mutual Funds?

Investing in mutual funds can be an excellent choice for many individuals seeking to grow their wealth over time. With numerous options available in the market, mutual funds present a broad range of advantages that make them appealing to investors, especially those who are new to investing or prefer a more hands-off approach. There are following reasons for investing in mutual funds:

1. Diversification

One of the primary reasons to invest in mutual funds is diversification. Diversification is the practice of spreading investments across a variety of assets to reduce the risk of a substantial loss. By pooling money from multiple investors, a mutual fund can invest in a broad spectrum of assets, including stocks, bond, real estate, commodities and international securities. This diversification helps in minimizing the impact of poor performance in any one investment.

For example, if you invest in a mutual fund, your money is typically distributed among numerous companies across different sectors. This means if one company or sector faces a downturn; it won't necessarily affect the entire fund. Diversification reduces the risk of losing all your capital due to poor performance in a single asset or sector. It's important to note that while diversification reduces risk, it does not eliminate it entirely, but it does make it more manageable for investors.

2. Professional Management

Mutual funds are managed by professional fund manager who have extensive expertise and experience in the financial markets. For individual investors who may lack the time, knowledge or resources to actively manage their investments, mutual funds offer a practical solution. Fund manager carefully select and monitor the assets within the fund, making trends and economic condition.

The presence of professional managers allows individual to benefit from their expertise. These fund managers often have access to tools and research that individual investors may not. Additionally, fund manager typically have the resources to make quick decision when necessary, adjusting the portfolio to adapt to changing market conditions. This level of professional management is not only convenient for the investor but also adds a layer of sophistication to the investment process.

3. Liquidity

Mutual funds offer high liquidity, meaning investors can buy or sell their shares easily, typically at the end of the trading day. This liquidity is an important factor to consider, as it allows investors to access their funds relatively quickly if they need cash for emergencies or other financial needs. Mutual funds provide daily pricing, allowing you to liquidate your investment on any business day, which is more advantageous than some other investment vehicles, such as real estate or certain bonds.

The ease of entering or exiting a mutual fund gives investors the flexibility to adjust their investment portfolios as their financial goals, risk tolerance or market conditions change. This makes mutual funds a more accessible and adaptable investment choice compared to less liquid assets.

4. Cost-Effectiveness

Mutual Funds are generally more cost-effective than managing a portfolio of individual securities, especially for small investors. For a relatively low minimum investment, you gain access to a diversified portfolio managed by professionals. Without mutual funds, investors would need to purchase multiple individual stocks or bonds to achieve similar diversification, which can be both time-consuming and costly due to transaction fees.

In addition to lower investment costs, mutual funds also benefit from economies of scale. Since they pool money from numerous investors, they can purchase assets in bulk, potentially lowering transaction costs and management fees. Moreover, many mutual funds allow you to invest with relatively low initial amounts, making them accessible to a wide range of investors.

5. Access to Different Asset Classes

Mutual funds provide easy access to different asset classes, including to those that may otherwise be difficult or expensive for individual investors to access. For example, many mutual funds invest in international markets, allowing investors to gain exposure to foreign economies without the complexity of dealing with currency exchanges or foreign market regulations. Similarly, there are mutual funds that focus on real estate, commodities and other asset classes that are difficult to access for retail investors.

Moreover, there are various types of mutual funds designed to meet specific investment goals, such as equity funds, bond funds, money market funds and hybrid funds. Each type of fund carries a different risk return profile making it easier for investors to select funds based on their personal preferences, financial goals and risk tolerance

6. Regulation and Safety

Mutual funds are subject to rigorous regulation by government authorities like the Securities and Exchange Board of India (SEBI) in India. These regulations are designed to protect investors by ensuring transparency, honesty and fairness in the way funds are managed. Fund managers are required to disclose all relevant information about the fund's performance, holding, fees and risks.

Furthermore, mutual funds are also required to have a custodian, an independent party that holds fund's assets. This reduces the risk of fraud or mismanagement and provides an additional layer of security to investors.

7. Rupee-Cost Averaging

Mutual fund offer investors the ability to implement a strategy known as Rupee-cost averaging. This strategy involves a fixed amount of money in a mutual fund at regular intervals, regardless of the market's performance. Over time, this approach can reduce the impact of short-term market fluctuations and lower the average cost of shares purchased.

By investing consistently over time, investors are less likely to be swayed by short-term market volatility or make emotional decisions based on market conditions. It allows investor to remain disciplined and steadily grow their portfolio without the need to time the market. This is particularly valuable for novice investors or those with long-term investor horizon.

8. Transparency and Reporting

Mutual funds are required to provide regular reports to their investors, offering a high level of transparency. Investors receive periodic updates on the fund's performance, holding and fees, ensuring they are well-informed about how their money is being managed.

Transparency helps to build trust between investors to assess the performance of their investments and ensure that the fund is adhering to its stated investment objectives

9. Long-Term Growth Potential

While mutual funds may not always provide the fastest short term gains, they are well-suited for long-term growth. The combination of diversification, professional management and access to various asset classes makes mutual funds an attractive option for individuals seeking to accumulate wealth over time. With the potential for capital appreciation, income generation and reinvestment, mutual funds can offer steady growth, particularly when held for an extended period.

In fact, the power of compounding can be significant when are reinvested, allowing for exponential growth over time. This is especially for investors with long term financial goal, such as retirement.

Points to Ponder before Investing in Mutual Funds

Before investing in mutual funds, It's essential to carefully consider various factors to ensure that your investment aligns with your financial goals, risk tolerance and overall strategy. Below are key points to keep in mind before making an investment in mutual funds:

1. Investment Goals

- **Define your Financial Objectives:** Are you investing for retirement, a down payment for a home, your children's education or another goal? Clearly defining your goals will help you to select the right type of mutual fund that aligns with your time horizon and expected returns.

- **Time Horizon:** Determine how long you plan to invest in the mutual fund. for example, if you have a long-term goal, you may require more conservative investments like bond funds or money market funds.

2. Risk Tolerance

- **Assess your Risk Appetite:** Different mutual funds come with varying degrees of risk. Equity funds (stocks) tend to be riskier but offer higher potential returns, while bond funds generally carry lower risk but provide more stable returns. Make sure you understand your tolerance for risk and choose a fund accordingly.

- **Diversification:** A well-diversified portfolio can help mitigate risk. Look for funds that diversify across multiple asset classes, industries and geographical regions.

3. Fund Type:

- **Understand the Different Types of Funds:** Mutual funds come in different categories, including equity funds, debt funds, hybrid funds, index funds, sector funds and international funds. Each type has its characteristics, risk level and investment strategy.

Choose a fund that align with your goals and risk profile.

- **Actively Managed vs Passively Managed Funds:** Actively managed funds have fund managers who make decisions on buying and selling assets, while passively managed funds (like index funds) track a specific market index. Actively managed funds generally have higher fees, but they may offer the potential for better returns.

4. **Fund Performance**

- **Examine Historical Performance:** Although past performance does not guarantee future returns, it can give you an idea of how the fund has performed in different market conditions. Look at the fund's long-term track record, especially over 5-10 years, to assess its consistency.

- **Compare with Benchmarks:** It's important to compare the fund's performance with a relevant benchmark.(eg Nifty 50 fund). This can help you determine whether the fund is outperforming or underperforming relative to the market.

5. **Expense Ratio and Fees**

- **Understanding the Costs:** Mutual funds charge various fees, including management fees, administrative fees and Exit load (when an investor redeems their mutual funds unit). The Expense ratio is the annual fee expressed as a percentage of the fund's assets. A lower expense ratio is generally better as high fees can erode returns over time.

- **Other Fees:** Be mindful of other charges such as redemption fees, exchange fees and account maintenance fees. Always read the prospectus to understand the full fee structure.

6. Fund Manager' s Experience and Reputation

- **Check the Fund Manager's track Record:** A skilled fund mange can make a significant difference in a mutual fund's performance. Research the fund's performance. Research the fund manager's history, experience and previous funds managed. Look for manager who have successfully navigate market cycles and have a consistent performance record.

- **Turnover Rate:** A high portfolio turnover rate can indicate active trading, which may result in higher costs and tax implications. If you prefer a more passive investment strategy, look for funds with lower turnover rates.

7. Fund Holdings

- **Understand where the Fund Invest in:** Review the fund's holding to ensure they align with your investment preference and risk tolerance. Some funds might heavily invest in certain sectors (eg technology, healthcare) or regions (e.g. emerging markets) which can expose you to sector specific or geographical risks.

- **Transparency:** Mutual funds should disclose their holdings regularly. Make sure the fund is transparent about where your money is being invested and consider whether that investment fit with your strategy.

8. Tax Implications

- **Understanding Tax Efficiency:** Mutual funds are subject to taxes on capital gains, dividends and interest income. Some funds are more tax-efficient than others. For example, tax-managed funds aim to minimize tax liabilities.

- **Short Term and Long Term Capital Gain:** Mutual funds are subject to short-term and long term capital gain.

9. Fund's Investment Strategy

- **Review the Fund's Investment Philosophy:** Look into the fund's prospectus to understand its investment strategy and objectives, Whether the fund focuses on growth, value, income generation or index tracking ensure it matches your financial goals

- **Risk Management Strategy:** Understand how the fund manages risk. Does it have a strategy for mitigating losses in downturns or does it focus on maximizing growth regardless of risk? Be sure that the fund's approach is in line with your risk tolerance and investment horizon.

10. Liquidity

- **Check Redemption and Withdrawal Terms:** While mutual funds are generally liquid, some funds may impose restriction or fees on withdrawals, especially if they are designed for long term investors. Ensure that the fund you select allows for easy access to your money if needed.

- **Exit Strategy:** If you are planning to invest for a specific time frame, make sure you understand the potential exit options, fees and penalties for early withdrawal.

11. Economic Conditions and Market Trends

- **Market Condition:** Keep in mind that economic conditions and market trends can impact mutual fund performance. For example, equity funds tend to perform well in a strong economic climate while bond funds might outperform in a low-interest rates. If rate rise, the value of existing bonds may decrease.

- **Interest Rate Sensitivity:** Bond funds, in particular are sensitive to change in interest rates. If rates rise, the value of existing bonds may decrease. Consider how macroeconomic factors may affect the fund you are invested in.

12. Review the Prospectus

- **Always Read the Prospectus:** The prospectus is a detailed document that provides information about the fund's objectives, strategies, risks, fees and performance. Reviewing the prospectus is critical before investing to ensure you fully understand what you are committing to.

13. Review and Ratings

- **Check Third-Party Ratings:** Organization like CRISIL, CARE, ICRA, SMERA and Brickwork Ratings provide independent reviews and rating of mutual funds based on factors such as performance, risk and fees.

- These rating can provide helpful insights into how a fund compares with its peers.

- **Investors Sentiment:** Look at reviews and feedback from other investors to get a sense of the fund's reputation and customer service. This can be particularly useful when dealing with larger fund management companies.

Investing in mutual fund can be an effective way to grow wealth, but it's important to carefully evaluate all aspects of the fund before investing. By considering factors like your financial goals, risk tolerance, investment horizon, fees and the fund's track record, you can make more informed decisions that align with your personal objectives. Taking the time to research and understand your option can help you build a strong and successful investment portfolio.

KEY TAKE AWAY

- Mutual Fund provide long term wealth creation

- Investors can start with a small amount

- Mutual funds automatically diversify your investment

- Investors benefit from the expertise of professional

- Mutual funds are highly regulated and transparent.

SYSTEMATIC WITHDRAWAL PLAN

"Investing is like planting a tree. A systematic withdrawal plan is how you ensure it provides fruit for years to come"

A Systematic Withdrawal Plan (SWP) is one of the most effective investment strategies that allow mutual fund investors to withdraw a fixed sum of money at regular intervals from their mutual fund investments.

This strategy is commonly used by individuals who seek to generate regular income stream, such as retirees or people who need a steady cash flow for meeting their expenses. SWP is the reverse of the Systematic Investment Plan (SIP), which involves investing fixed amount periodically in mutual funds.

The way SWP works is simple: An investor sets up the withdrawal amount and the mutual fund manager will redeem units periodically to generate the necessary cash flow. This arrangement helps investors maintain a disciplined approach to withdrawals and can be adjusted as per the investor.

While SWP ensures that an investor continues to receive income, it does not necessarily liquidate the entre mutual fund corpus.

The units in the mutual fund continue to appreciate and the remaining units still have the potential to grow based on the performance of the mutual fund.

1. **Features of SWP in Mutual Funds**

- **Fixed Withdrawals:** The most important feature of an SWP is the fixed amount that the investor can withdraw at predetermined intervals. This can be fixed percentage of the total corpus depending on the needs of the investors.

- **Flexible Frequency:** Another important feature is the flexible in choosing the frequency of withdrawals. Typically, an investor can choose to receive their withdrawal monthly, quarterly or annually. The frequency depends on the investor's goals, such as covering monthly expenses or making periodic investments elsewhere.

- **Regular and Predictable Income:** For retirees and those looking to supplement their income, SWP offers the benefit of predictability and consistency. Knowing the amount that will be withdrawal at regular intervals gives the investor peace of mind and ensures steady cash flow.

- **Capital Appreciation:** Even after the withdrawal, the remaining mutual fund units in the investor account continue to appreciate according to the market movements. The investor does not need to sell off all their units at once. Instead, they can keep the remaining units invested, allowing them to grow over time. Thus, SWP allows the best of both words-

regular withdrawals while still having potential for growth.

- **Tax Implication:** The tax treatment of SWP depends on the type of mutual fund from which the withdrawal is made. For instance, equity mutual funds are subject to capital gains tax and the tax rate varies depending on how long the investors have held units.

- **Rupee Cost Averaging:** When SWP is used, there is a concept similar to rupee cost averaging (RCA). If the mutual fund's net asset value (NAV) fluctuates, the number of units redeemed will vary accordingly. This reduces the impact of short-term market volatility because the redemption will happen at different NAVs over time

2. Types of Mutual Funds Suitable for SWP

Different types of mutual funds can be used in SWPs. Depending on the investor's risk appetite, financial goals and time horizon. Here are the types of funds commonly used for SWP:

- **Equity Mutual Funds:** Equity mutual funds invest primarily in stocks and are considered high-risk, high-return investment. They are suitable for investors who are looking for higher capital appreciation and are willing to accept the volatility associated with the stock market. Over the long term, equity funds generally outperform other asset classes, but they may not be as stable in the short term. Therefore, investors who use equity funds for SWP must have risk tolerance.

- **Debt Mutual Fund:** Debt mutual funds invest in fixed-income instruments such as bonds, government securities and money market instruments. These funds are less volatile compared to equity funds, making them suitable for risk-averse investors. Debt funds typically offer lower returns than equity funds but provide a more predictable and stable income stream. They are idea for conservative investors or those looking for stable, regular income.

- **Hybrid Mutual Funds:** Hybrid funds invest in a mix of equity and debt securities. These funds aim to provide a balanced portfolio with both capital appreciation and income generation. Hybrid funds can be an excellent option for investors who want a moderate risk level and a combination of income generation. These funds provide an intermediate solution between equity and debt funds, making them more versatile for SWP purposes.

- **Liquid funds:** Liquid funds are a type of debt mutual fund that primarily invests in short-term instruments with a low duration. These funds are designed to provide liquidity funds can be good option for an SWP, as they are less affected by interest rate fluctuations.

3. Pros and Cons of SWP

Pros:

- **Regular Income:** The primarily benefit of an SWP is that it provides a steady stream of income, which is particularly useful for retirees or anyone looking for a reliable source of income. The fixed withdrawals help to ensure that the investors can cover their living expenses without worrying about selling investments.

- **Capital Appreciation Potential:** Unlike other traditional income-generating investments, SWP allows the investor's remaining corpus to continue growing as long as the mutual fund performs well. Even as the investor withdrawal funds,, the remaining amount has the potential to generate returns.

- **Rupee Cost Averaging:** Rupee cost averaging helps to reduce the negative impact of market volatility, which is crucial in volatile market conditions. Since the units are redeemed over time, it smooths out the effect of market fluctuations.

- **Flexible and Customizable:** SWP is highly customizable, allowing the investor to adjust the withdrawal amount and frequency as per their financial needs. Moreover, if the investor's requirements change, the plan can be attended or stopped entirely.

- **Automate and Hassle-Free:** Once set up, an SWP runs automatically without requiring frequent intervention from the investor. This makes it a hassle–free way to generate regular income. It eliminates the need to monitor market conditions and decide when to redeem units.

- **Discipline in Withdrawals:** The structured nature of SWP helps investors follow a discipline approach in withdrawing funds. Investors can avoid the temptation of withdrawing large sum during market rallies or panic selling during downturns.

Cons:

- **Risk of Diminishing Capital:** One of the key risks of SWP is that regular withdrawals can erode the investor's principal, especially if the market does not perform well or if the withdrawal amount is too high. If the mutual fund underperforms, the investors might end up with a smaller corpus over time, which could affect future withdrawals.

- **No Guaranteed Returns:** SWP does not guarantee any fixed returns; The amount that the investors receives depends on the performance of the mutual fund. While debt funds are more stable, even they can be impacted by changes in interest rate, inflation and economic conditions.

- **Inflation Risk:** The fixed amount withdrawn through SWP may not keep up with inflation. Over time, the purchasing power of the withdrawn amount will decline if inflation rises. Hence, if the withdrawal amount is not adjusted for inflation, the investor's income might not be sufficient to meet future needs.

- **No Control Over Market Conditions:** Although the investor has control over the amount and frequency of withdrawals, the market conditions are outside their control. If the market experiences a downturn, it can negatively affect the mutual fund's NAV and consequently, the value of the withdrawals.

- **Premature Depletion of Capital:** If the investors continue to withdraw money regularly without considering market performance or adjustments in withdrawal amounts, there is a risk of exhausting the investment corpus prematurely. This is particularly concerning for retirees who depend on their investments for long-term income.

4. **How to Set Up an SWP**

Setting up an SWP is a relatively simple process. Here are the steps involved:

- **Select a Mutual Fund:** Choose a mutual fund that aligns with your risk tolerance, goals and investment horizon.

- **Complete KYC:** Complete the KYC process which is mandatory before investing in mutual funds.

- **FILL Out SWP form**: You need to fill out the SWP mandate form which includes the amount you wish to withdraw the frequency of withdrawals and the mutual fund scheme from which you want to withdraw.

- **Submit the form:** Submit the SWP form along with necessary documents to the mutual fund house. The request can be submitted online or physically.

- **Monitor the Withdrawals:** Once the SWP is set up, monitor the withdrawals and make adjustment as required.

5. How SWP works?

A Systematic Withdrawal Plan (SWP) allows an investor to withdraw a fixed amount regularly while the remaining corpus continue to grow based on specified annual return. In this example, you have a corpus of Rs 30,00,000, and you are withdrawing Rs 25,000 every month. The corpus grows at an annual rate of 12% compounded monthly.

Assumption:

- Initial corpus: Rs 30,00,000

- Monthly withdrawal: Rs 25,000

- Annual growth rate: 12% (which is 1% per month)

- Monthly interest: Corpus $\times$ 0.01 (i,e 12 % annual return divided by 12 months)

Example Table:

Month	Starting Corpus (₹)	Interest Earned (₹)	Withdrawal (₹)	Ending Corpus (₹)
1	30,00,000	30,000	25,000	30,05,000
2	30,05,000	30,050	25,000	30,10,050
3	30,10,050	30,100	25,000	30,15,150
4	30,15,150	30,151	25,000	30,20,301
5	30,20,301	30,203	25,000	30,25,504
6	30,25,504	30,255	25,000	30,30,759

Explanation:

- **Starting Corpus (Rs):** The amount of money in the corpus at the beginning of each month.

- **Interest Earned (Rs):** The interest earned on the corpus for that month, calculated at 1% per month (12% annually).

- **Withdrawal (Rs):** The fixed withdrawal amount, which is Rs 25,000 each month.

- **Ending Corpus (Rs):** The remaining corpus after the interest earned and the withdrawal. This is calculated as:

Ending Corpus= (Starting Corpus + Interest Earned) – Withdrawal

How it Works:

- Each month, you withdraw Rs 25,000.

- The remaining corpus continues to earn interest at the rate of 1% per month.

- The ending corpus after each month is starting corpus plus the interest earned, minus the withdrawal.

This process continues, and the corpus keeps growing due to the monthly interest earned, although the withdrawal reduces the corpus over time.

If investor can analyze what is systematic withdrawal plan in mutual fund, they will find that SWP is a good strategy to have a regular income with some sort of regularity.

A SWP can also be set up to withdraw only the capital appreciation portion. The good part is that the returns are tax efficient and there is no TDS on gains unlike traditional investment options.

KEY TAKE AWAY

- SWP provides a regular income

- Your corpus continues to grow based on the return of your investment

- There is a risk of exhausting the corpus if the withdrawals exceed the returns

- Ideal for retirement planning

- It provides flexibility in withdrawal

The Debt Trap

"Debt is the worst poverty"

—Thomas Fuller

India, a nation of over 1.4 billion people, faces a diverse set of economic challenges. One of the most pressing issues confronting the country is the prevalence of a "debt trap." A debt trap refers to a situation where individuals or households borrow money to fulfill immediate financial needs or desires but struggle to repay the borrowed amount, eventually becoming trapped in an unending cycle of borrowing.

Debt traps are particularly dangerous because they can lead to severe financial distress, social disintegration, and long-term economic instability.

In India, both rural and urban populations have been affected by this problem, which is further exacerbated by rising inflation, inadequate financial literacy, and a lack of structured financial regulations.

In a 2021 survey, it was found that around **42% of rural households** borrowed from informal sources, primarily local moneylenders, due to their easy accessibility. However, the problem with informal lending is the lack of regulation, and the high-interest rates force many borrowers into a cycle of debt that is impossible to escape.

1. **Causes of Debt Traps**

- **Access to Easy Digital Loans:** With the rise of digital lending platforms, borrowing money has become increasingly easy. In India, apps such as PaySense, CashBean, and KreditBee have flooded the market, providing loans with minimal documentation and quick disbursal. While these platforms offer the convenience of borrowing, they come with high-interest rates, hidden fees, and unregulated practices.

- **Low Financial Literacy:** A major cause of debt traps in India is the low level of financial literacy. In rural areas, financial education is minimal, and many people do not fully understand the terms and conditions of loans, interest rates, or the implications of taking on debt.

According to a study by the **National Centre for Financial Education (NCFE), about 27% of Indian adults** are financially illiterate. In rural India, where people rely on informal lending, this lack of financial knowledge can lead to a situation where borrowers do not realize how their loans will accumulate interest over time or the impact of missing payments.

- **Cultural Expectations and Social Pressures:** In India, social pressures to maintain certain lifestyle standards, particularly in relation to weddings, festivals, and education, often push families into taking on debt.

Cultural expectations around lavish weddings, expensive gifts, and extravagant celebrations force families to borrow money, which they cannot repay.

According to the National Sample Survey (NSS) 2018 report, the average expenditure on weddings in India is estimated at ₹5 lakh ($6,500), with many families borrowing significant amounts to meet the expectations of grand celebrations.

In many cases, the heavy financial burden leads to individuals borrowing further to pay off earlier debts, trapping them in a vicious cycle.

- **Economic Instability and Inflation:** Economic instability, inflation, and rising costs of living also contribute to the debt trap. Over the years, inflation in India has pushed up the prices of essential commodities, making it harder for families to make ends meet. According to **India's Consumer Price Index (CPI)**, food inflation has increased by **6-8%** annually in recent years, significantly affecting household budgets.

In such circumstances, many families resort to borrowing to cover day-to-day expenses, leading to an accumulation of debt.

The situation worsens when there is an economic slowdown, resulting in job losses or salary cuts, forcing individuals to borrow more and further entrenching the cycle.

2. **Consequences of Debt Traps**

The consequences of debt traps are far-reaching, impacting individuals, families, and the broader economy.

- **Reduced Savings and Investment**: As individuals use their income to pay off debt, their ability to save or invest diminishes. According to the **World Bank**, India's household savings rate has fallen from **23% in 2010** to just **17% in 2021**, largely because people are diverting their income toward debt repayment.

- **Loss of Assets**: Many people, particularly farmers and rural households, end up losing assets such as land, cattle, or property when they fail to repay their loans. The **All India Debt and Investment Survey 2018-19** revealed that approximately **50% of rural households** are in debt, with land being used as collateral to secure loans, leading to the sale of assets in cases of default.

- **Debt-Related Stress**: The psychological impact of debt is severe. Many individuals experience anxiety, depression, and social stigma due to their inability to repay loans. This has been linked to an increasing number of suicides, particularly in rural areas. The **National Crime Records Bureau (NCRB)** reports that **about 10,000 farmers** commit suicide annually in India, with debt being one of the key reasons behind these tragic events.

- **Breakdown of Families**: The pressure to repay debts often leads to strained family relationships. Borrowers are forced to take extreme steps, including selling off family assets or engaging in unhealthy borrowing practices, which can result in emotional and social breakdowns.

3. Breaking the Debt Trap: Potential Solutions

Tackling the issue of debt traps requires a holistic approach involving financial education, regulation of lending practices, and greater access to affordable credit.

a) Assess your Financial Situation

- **List All Debts:** The first step is to get a clear picture of your financial situation. List all your debts, including credit card debts, personal loans, mortgages and liabilities. Include details like the total amount owed, interest rates, minimum monthly payments and due dates.

- **Calculate your Total Debts:** Understanding the total amount of debt you owe will help you to evaluate the magnitude of the situation and set realistic goals for repayment.

b) Create a Budget

- **Track Income and Expenses:** Create a detailed monthly budget to track your income and expenses. This helps you identify areas where you can cut back on non-essential spending and allocate more towards debt repayment.

- **Prioritize Spending:** Focus on necessities like food, utilities and housing. Avoid unnecessary luxuries until the debt is under control.

- **Avoid Additional Debt:** Temporarily stop using credit cards or taking on new loans. Any new debt will only make the situation worse.

c) Negotiate with Creditors

- **Talk to Your Lenders:** Reach out to your lenders and explain your situation. Many lenders are open to negotiating lower interest rates, extended repayment terms or even temporarily suspending payments if you are facing financial hardship.

- **Consolidation   or   Refinancing:**   consider consolidating multiple debts into a single loan with a lower interest rates or refinancing high-interest loans to reduce monthly payments.

- **Debt Settlement:** If you are unable to repay the full amount, some creditors may willing to accept a lower lump-sum settlement. This is typically more beneficial if your financial situation is dire.

d) Cut Unnecessary Expenses

- **Eliminate Non-Essential Spending:** Temporarily cut back on discretionary spending like entertainment, dining out and impulse purchases. This will free up more funds to put forward paying off debt.

- **Downsize:** If possible, consider downsizing your lifestyle. This could mean moving to a smaller home, selling unused assets or finding cheaper alternatives for services and goods.

e) Increase Your Income

- **Find Additional Sources of Income:** Look for side jobs, freelancing opportunities or part-time work to increase your income. This can provide extra money that can be used to pay off debt faster.

- **Sell Unused Assets:** If you have valuable items like electronics, furniture or collectibles that you no longer need. Consider selling them to raise funds for debt repayment.

f) Build an Emergency Funds

- **Save for Emergencies:** While it may seem counterintuitive when you are in debt, having a small emergency fund (such as Rs10,000 – Rs20,000) can prevent you from falling deeper into debt due to unexpected expenses. This fund will help you avoid relying on credit cards or loans during emergencies.

g) Develop Financial Discipline

- **Avoid New Debt:** One of the key aspects of getting out of debt trap is breaking the cycle of borrowing.

Make a commitment to avoid taking on new loans, using credit cards or relying on borrowing until you are debt-free.

- **Live Within Your Means:** Moving forward, focus on living within your means and adopting responsible spending habits. Avoid impulse purchases, create a long-term saving plan and only borrow money when absolutely necessary.

h) Monitor You Progress Regularly

- **Track Your Debt Reduction:** Regularly monitor your progress towards paying off your debt. This will give you a sense of accomplishment as you see the balance decrease.

- **Reevaluate Your Budget:** Occasionally reassess your budget and make adjustments based on any change in your financial situation, such as increased income or reduced expenses.

i) Stay Positive and Patient

- **Maintain a Positive Mindset:** Getting out of a debt trap is a gradual process and it requires patience and perseverance. Stay motivated and keep your long-term financial goal in mind.

- **Celebrate Small Wins:** Each time you pay off debts or make significant progress, take a moment to celebrate. Acknowledgement small victories can keep you motivated on the path to full financial recovery.

Escaping a debt trap is challenging but with the right approach, it is entirely possible. The key to take proactive steps- assess your situation, make a solid repayment plan, reduce expenses and increase income. Furthermore, seeking help from professionals, such as financial counselors or debt management services can provide invaluable guidance during the process. By adopting better financial habits and developing discipline, you can not only get out of the debt trap but also build a secure financial future.

KEY TAKE AWAY

- Track your income and expenses to understand where your money is going

- Focus on paying off high-interest debts (like credit cards)

- Build an emergency fund

- Increase income and cut unnecessary expenses

- Stay consistent and patient

Disclaimer

The content of this book, *Refine Your Finance*, is provided for general informational purposes only. While the author has made every effort to ensure the accuracy and reliability of the information presented, this book should not be construed as financial, legal, or investment advice. The strategies, tips, and suggestions offered are based on general principles and personal experience and may not be suitable for every individual or financial situation.

Financial decisions are personal, and each person's circumstances may differ. Readers are strongly encouraged to conduct their own research and seek advice from qualified financial, legal, and tax professionals before making any decisions related to budgeting, insurance, loans, credit cards, real estate, or any other financial matters discussed in this book.

The author and publisher do not accept any responsibility for any actions taken or decisions made based on the information provided in this book. The use of any information in this book is solely at your own risk. Past performance does not guarantee future results, and there are always inherent risks involved in financial planning and investing.

Furthermore, this book does not endorse any specific product, service, or financial institution. Any references to particular companies, products, or services are for illustrative purposes only and do not constitute an endorsement or recommendation.

By using this book, you acknowledge and agree to the terms of this disclaimer. The author and publisher disclaim all liability for any loss or damage arising from your reliance on the information contained herein.

ABOUT THE AUTHOR

J KHAN, The author of ***Refine Your Finance*** is a passionate advocate for creating financial literacy and empowering individuals to make informed decisions about their money.

With over 20 years of investment experience, ranging from traditional fixed deposits (FDs) to the dynamic world of crypto currencies.

The author emphasizes the importance of building wealth to beat inflation and achieve long-term financial success. With a keen focus on avoiding the debt trap, a strong believer in the power of financial education.

MAY I ASK YOU FOR A SMALL FAVOR?

First, I want to thank you for reading this book. You could have chosen any other book, but you took mine, and I appreciate this. I hope you have at least a few actionable insights that will positively impact your daily life.

Can I ask for 30 seconds more of your time?

I'd love it if you could leave a review of the book. That will help me grow my readership by encouraging folks to take a chance on my books.

Keeping it straight - reviews are the lifeblood of any author.

It will take less than a minute of your time but will tremendously help me reach out to more people.

If you liked this book, please consider posting an honest review on your preferred retailer. And I'd love to see your review. Thanks for your support.